D0590523

THE TRAVELLER'S
BEDSIDE BOOK

Edward Hyams

With contributions by
MARY BACON

FABER AND FABER
London

First published in 1970
by Faber and Faber Limited
24 Russell Square London WC1
Printed in Great Britain by
W. & J. Mackay & Co Ltd, Chatham
All rights reserved

ISBN 0 571 08299 8

FOR VICTORIA
with love from both of us

Acknowledgments

Thanks are due to the following publishers and authors for permission to quote from the works listed:

Spanish Fare by André Marling (Cassell & Co. Ltd.); *The Irrational Journey* by Pauline de Rothschild (Hamish Hamilton Ltd.); *The Heart of Iran* by Duncan Forbes (Robert Hale & Co.); *Prospero's Cell* by Lawrence Durrell (Faber & Faber Ltd.); *Hill Towns of Italy* by Lilian Notestein (Hutchinson & Co. (Publishers) Ltd.).

And to the *New Statesman*, in which one or two of these pieces first appeared.

E.H.

Contents

7

Contents

Contents

9

Contents

Contents

Humanism in Italy

'You are going to Sicily?' said my Milanese friend, 'I am sorry for you; it is the only country I know where the fat bourgeois is even more surly and uncouth than the starved peasant.' He brooded and added: 'But the rest of Italy—it is no longer a good country to live in.' Non-Italian, he has lived and worked in Italy, made a modest fortune even, for a third of a lifetime. Why, I asked, such gloom? I still liked it there, though I did not have to live in it: 'It is a country which is being fouled and destroyed by its own inhabitants.' I said that that was happening everywhere. 'Of course, but much worse here.' He led me to the window and pointed in silence to the permanent and thickening traffic jam and I was, in my turn, silent. If it were only Milan . . . but Rome, which survived the Goths and the Huns, and the French, Germans, English and Americans, is being destroyed by the motor-car makers and their customers, including myself. I shifted my friend from the generalities at which he is no better, after all, than the rest of us, to his own subject: it seems that if the young writer in Britain thinks his lot a hard one, he should consider that of his Italian counterpart and, like the saved looking down on the tortures of the damned in hell, rejoice like a Christian. The Italian aspirant to a bare living (and never mind success) in imaginative literature has not the Englishman's, say, fifty chances of a publisher before he gives up and takes to advertising, but eight at most. More than 80 per cent of Italian publishing is owned by five big firms each directed by a million-aire whose dream is less of discovering a real writer than of next year's extra hundred million lire on the takings. Paperbacks?

13

Three of them have paperback subsidiaries, but nobody can have a really big one, because, each hating the other like poison, none will grant a licence to any other. These big five, beloved of their bankers, but less by their authors, depend chiefly on translations. There is a new and goodish school of novelists whom their own publishers disdain for failing to be American or French, but who have one strength: poor native work always sells better than good translation of good foreign work. Book-buying is on the increase, but only in proportion to the increase in population and in literacy.

The fact seems to be that Italian humanism is now, as in the beginning, expressing itself more in the design of objects for use than in the ornaments of life. Motor-cars and, above all, the new roads, blocks of flats for workers and lower middle-class, whether in Piedmont or Sicily, new houses, clothes and shoes are better designed and better made than ours; TV advertising is less bad than ours. It is true that pop singing is much worse, but then it is not a native art. But in the fine arts at the lower level, the kitsch is atrocious: compare the kind of paintings which sell merely to cover wallspace; ours are feeble, but the Italian examples are foul, as if painted in coloured treacle.

Plain, Blunt Russians

Much has been written about the grey dismalness of the Soviet urban scene. In the south it's cured by trees, which the Russians love and plant in vast numbers, and by flowers. But even there, and much more so in the northern cities, there are three obvious causes of the prevailing grimness: lack of grace in the design of things; lack of skill and materials in the newest and showiest of the applied arts—window-dressing; and total absence of advertisements. Say what you like about the corrupting and cynical unscrupulousness of advertising and shop-window salesmanship, at least it turns cities without architectural graces into vast pop-art galleries which are lively and colourful. Colour, or rather want of it, is a fourth cause; either Russians are colour-shy, colour-blind, or they have very bad dyes. But it is the clumsy and amateurish design which is most apparent. Anciently, many of the hundred nationalities of the Soviet Union made very pretty things; that some of them still can do so is manifest in the expensive luxury goods sold only in the special foreign-currency shops. But for the most part the talent for good design must have become latent, because there's not a sign of it in the clothes, motor-cars, motor-scooters, gadgets. In machinery the fault is not fundamental; Soviet motor-cars have a perfectly adequate performance, even rather better than that, and they appear to be massively resistant to hard driving on indifferent roads; but they look ugly. It could be a manifestation of the ruling puritanism, but I don't think so. I think it's plain ineptitude, like the surliness of Soviet manners, which is not the expression of ill-will which it seems, but a kind of awkwardness. My travelling companion, Yorkshire born and bred, was repeatedly reminded of North Country plain-blunt-mannery; but by no means always and in everything, for example on the three or four occasions when she had her hand kissed or was given flowers. For my part, it was Australia that Soviet manners put me in mind of.

Fountains

The little art of fountains has long been in decline; there's a beauty in Sydney, a huge puff-ball of hundreds of jets composing a water-sphere: and, of course, the very lovely inverted fountain in that superb architectural masterpiece, the Museum of Anthropology in Mexico City. But only in the late Pierre du Pont's Longwood, Pennsylvania, is there a great battery of fountains, composing a complex and repeatedly changing play of scores of jets, to compare with such ornamental waterworks as the Villa d'Este's or the Villa Lante's. Longwood is supposed to be the place where the witticism, since become a cliché, 'Think what God would have done if he'd had money', was originated by a departing visitor. In two respects the Longwood fountains surpass the Italian Renaissance ones and those of the Andalusian Moorish palaces: in volume and power of jets, and in the new minor art of our century, floodlighting. At night the vast panorama of changing water-patterns, of great jets growing as others decline, jets crossing, broadening, narrowing, tossing, falling, rising, is illuminated by a twenty-minute sequence of changing colours and colour combinations. The spectacle is as thrilling and pretty and diverting as a grand firework display (another vanishing minor art). Beside me in the crowd on the grand terrace in front of the huge Victorian-style conservatories, a clear and unmistakably English voice said, 'How unspeakably vulgar.' Well, yes, no doubt—exactly as vulgar as the so-called musical fountains of the sixteenth-century Italian tycoons, as the Owl Fountain at the Villa d'Este, which hooted, the Organ Fountain of which Montaigne complained that it had but one note, and the Dragon Fountain which delighted John Evelyn by roaring at him.

Cinema in Kiev

Maybe talent for graphic arts in the USSR goes into film-making. Russians take their cinema-going seriously and a hard seat in a bleak hall perfectly designed for good viewing costs R.1.50 (15s, with wages and salaries much lower than ours). Our visit to the cinema in Kiev was to see the new *Anna Karenina*, and it was a notable experience to sit through a movie so good that one was utterly absorbed for more than two hours despite not understanding more than one word in ten of the dialogue. The acting is superlative, sets beautifully authentic, costumes just sufficiently *outré* to make the vital difference between a work of art and a sort of documentary-of-a-novel. The film is visually enchanting, the use of colour restrained. The country scenes are more powerfully evocative of the singular charm of Russia's flat immensity than anything I have seen before; and one sequence, in a birchwood at autumn, more beautiful than anything I have seen on the screen. In the outdoor set-pieces— the steeplechase which ends with Vronsky savagely kicking and flogging his horse for coming down at a jump and breaking its back; and a croquet game—there is a pleasing touch of formal staginess borrowed from ballet. If the film is released outside the Soviet Union and is dubbed I hope they'll allow the actors to speak the short passages of French dialogue with a better accent: in my experience Russians speak French very prettily; for some reason—an ideological irony?—they're made to speak it in the film with a coarse Russian accent.

Greek Temples and Australian Wattles

Try as I will, I cannot be deeply impressed by Greek temples. In the low light of morning or evening I can be moved by the thought of all the people who worshipped at them and who, having thought, like us, that they would live for ever, died all the same. But as architecture, the temples have a blockish stockiness which by comparison with the religious architecture of our own great period lacks lightness, lacks the quality of soaring, of space briefly trapped in the minimum of stone line. Still, by becoming ruins, the temples at Paestum and Agrigento have achieved grace, especially at Agrigento and by virtue of the magnificent siting. But isn't it curious that our humanists, striving for centuries to destroy western Christian superstition, were and remain the first to revere these monuments to a superstition at least as gross as ours? And who, I wonder in the name of Erasmus and all the Hellenists, is responsible for planting Australian wattles about the temples which can only really strike the right note in the nostalgic scale when seen among olives and figs and vines and cypresses? Mimosa, of all things!

And yet, on second thoughts, why not? Because of a long series of very successful plant introductions, of southern baroque architecture, above all of tree-felling on a catastrophic scale, the Mediterranean landscape we know is nothing whatever like the classical landscape, the landscape which the Greek colonists of Sicily and Southern Italy first looked at, and built their temples in. So, after all why not mimosa? It's rather less offensive about Greek temples than the horrible floribunda roses which disfigure hundreds of English chapter and cathedral gardens.

Monuments in Russia

Unlike the dreary hideousness of Soviet monumental, factory and domestic architecture, I don't believe that the poverty of Soviet graphic art was ever attributable simply to the Stalinist blight, any more than it can now be attributed to the blimpish, academic conservatism, perfectly comparable with the British version until quite recently, of the people in power. Did the Russians ever have painters and sculptors of the first or even second rate? Early church painting is poor Byzantine. Later epochs produced poor Italian and poor French derivatives. Monumental art was always pretty terrible and it still is: where it's realistic like the Potemkin memorial in Odessa, it has no strength, despite massiveness, to compensate for want of grace; and where it's 'modern', as it sometimes is now, all it achieves is a demonstration of Soviet skill in casting large masses of concrete. I don't believe you can draw any conclusions about Soviet art from this, only about Russian art; these arts have never, as far as I could see, been 'proper' to Russian culture in the sense that poetry, the novel, dancing, music and even architecture have been. In architecture, supposing the academic conservatism of communism can be relaxed, there's hope of a revival of the fancy which made the old church architecture so charming, and which is manifest in the early 19th century baroque of Kievan domestic architecture, and of the same period in odd corners of Minsk and quarters of Moscow. From the look of some of the new apartment blocks—enormous numbers of these wherever we went—and especially in the Ukraine, the dismal era of the worst kind of Stalinist brutishness in building is over. One must not expect too much in a country governed by aesthetic caution and priggishness, the one great country left where youth is at a heavy discount; there is none of the distinction one sees in Italy, none of the boldness of Brazil or Mexico, no really amusing tricks with concrete and steel.

But there is a little return to fanciful decoration, for example in the Khirghiz contribution to the rebuilding of Tashkent which was largely destroyed in an earthquake in 1963; and in Kiev the new housing blocks have some of the lightness and colour which you can see in any Italian rehousing scheme, and even in Deptford, London. I can't see anyone putting up any more of the burly, ill-proportioned and entirely hideous porticos—a sort of monstrous blow-up of the rather pretty 19th century Russian Classical style—which disgraced the Fifties. True, there's nothing specifically 'Soviet', nothing original except the decorative touches, about even the best of the new buildings; on the other hand they are no longer worse than they are in other parts of the world.

Horse cabs as tourist bait

I suppose we have now driven a motor-car in most countries. There are some, such as Indonesia and Persia, where the penalties for foreigners who transgress the law are so heavy that it is wise to be driven. But always there is the thought, 'How nice it would be to drive in a horse and carriage'. The pace is slower, there is more opportunity for seeing the countryside, or the town sights, the rhythm is pleasant and so on.

One of the most frightening drives we ever took was in Rome; we engaged a horse and rather high carriage to see the sights; we climbed up on the passenger seat, which seemed very high up in the air, and off we went. Unfortunately we had reckoned without the push and thrust of the normal Roman traffic, little FIATS came within an inch of our wheels; VESPAS dodged under the horse's head, causing him to trot with his nose well tucked into his shoulder, and the driver to flick him gently with his whip and talk to him in a soothing shout. And then the *pavé*; in a car one forgets how much of Rome is still paved with cobbles. We are both reasonably thin and the seat was designed for large bums, or more charitably for three people; however, we bounced up and down and side to side and by the time we arrived back at our favourite drinking place, the Piazza Navona, our nerves were well shattered.

In Palermo the *carrozze* are not a tourist trap but part of the taxi service of the town: they have meters and are rather cheaper than a motor taxi. A friend of ours, who was foolish enough to argue with a taxi driver about the price of a very short ride, found himself 'blacked' by the motor taxi drivers outside his hotel and he appealed to us for help. We put him into a *carrozza*, he made good time for his appointment and subsequently he used no other means of transport.

In Naples the cabbies are all Jehus and the horses are all martyrs. Unless a clear understanding as to price and time of journey is reached, you may find that you have an impassioned argument in Neapolitan Italian to cope with. But there again, as in Palermo, the carriages are comfortable, although the horses are never as sleek and well looked after.

We were once in the maddening position of having six hours to spend on Corfu, arriving on a passenger-cargo boat at five in the morning. We wanted to see everything and almost succeeded but found that we were far away from the dock at 11 a.m. So we hailed a horse and carriage and, mercifully, the cabby spoke a little English and some French—he had been in the late war— and when we explained the situation, gave him the name of the ship and became slightly hysterical over whatever awful fate befell tourists who were late on board, his whole face lit up and he said, 'Lady, gentleman, we go very fast . . .' And we did; he whipped up his horse, we clung on to the sides of the carriage as he lashed out with his whip at motor cyclists, pedestrians, cars and anything that came between us and the dock. As we had exaggerated the time through nervousness, our arrival was dramatic, especially as he leapt down and shouted up to the ship's officer who was idly taking the going-ashore cards from a number of decorous people coming up the gangway, that the ship must not move until we were on board; as there seemed no possibility of this happening for at least ten minutes there was a bit of an anti-climax.

Customs in Boston

Arrived by Flight BOAC 561 Logan Airport, Boston, Mass. We passed through customs—the US Customs are among the few left in the world, with the Brazilian and Indonesian, who take this nonsense seriously; so our cases were opened. On our way out with a porter to find a taxi, I was stopped by a young man in civilian clothes, who showed a badge—US Customs—and required us to accompany him and answer a few questions. He was very taken aback when Mary showed an inclination to resist, under the impression that this was some sort of 'con'. (If you've been to the US a few times there is a kind of feeling, difficult to suppress, that the police are also a kind of criminal.) We were taken, with porter and luggage, to an office. I was inclined to be resentful and asked for an explanation: 'You're a very slim man, Mr Hyams, but from the back you look kind of bulky.' They suspected my clothes of concealing contraband. I was required to turn out my pockets, while they kept asking Mary to 'Have a seat, Ma'am,' to which she answered frostily and bristling like an angry kitten that she preferred to stand. Finding nothing on me—I hate carrying anything but the flattest papers in my pockets—they wanted to know if Mary's blue and jonquil

sapphire ring was intended as a present for anyone in the States.
'Good God, no'.

'But it'd make a handsome gift, ma'am'.

'That's what I thought when it was given to me'.

The conversation between the officers was cryptic. One asked
the other if Mary was 'on the same deck' as me. Apparently not.
They were polite, awkward, not sure what they were doing; and,
of course, ridiculous. Later, I asked a Boston friend what they
were looking for and he said 'Heroin. This is the biggest port of
entry for it in America'.

'But why pick on me?'

'You have a beard'.

Motorcar mœurs

In Europe people have cars. In the United States cars have
people; or almost. Certainly, the motor-car in America is not
the same kind of possession as it is in Britain. We have cars the
way we have golf-clubs or, at a more serious level, slide-rules.
In America they have cars the way they have legs. I have had a
nightmare which makes me think this distinction is important;
automan. Important, because the mechanization of man to make
automan may be, in part, responsible for some other differences
between the American and the British way of life. A mechanism,
however sophisticated, is less flexible than an organism:
automan is half mechanism, half organism; his outline is firmer
than a man's, his place more necessarily predetermined. He
tends to be one of a model rather than an individual. Hence the
tendency of the income-bracket system to harden into a caste
system: for a Chevrolet is a Chevrolet, a Cadillac a Cadillac.

Don't dismiss automan as merely a nightmare: he exists, he is different. Man, *Homo sapiens*, has a natural speed of movement of between three and 20 m.p.h.; the speed at which automan thinks of himself as moving is 60 m.p.h. And automan will prosper; he is a viable species; he is predictable as man is not, and easy to govern.

It is very hard to resist turning into an automan over there. I have been taking turns at the wheel with my friend George on a long drive out of New York. I have been driving for 40 years but at the wheel I am a man self-consciously and deliberately operating a machine. George, on his feet, is still the most human of men. But as he gets behind the wheel a curious and subtle change takes place. He does not, like me, have to *attend*, he simply becomes an organ of the symbiotic creature automan, his actions responding to a nervous system which is a fusion of his own and the car's.

When we shrug our shoulders at the great size, the romantic outline and trim of the American cars, and reproach the American motor-industry with selling not a tool but rather a knight's charger or a gun-and-chaps substitute, we are being very superficial in our criticism. For it is not that General Motors are guilty of charming money out of their customers by inflating their egos. The ego is demanding that its new body be such as will fittingly accommodate and express the broad, though shallow, automan soul.

Although many Britons and other Europeans are, of course, automen—usually these are third- or at least second-generation owner-drivers—most are not and Americans do not always understand that foreigners are not fully metamorphosed, which can cause much confusion. There was, for example, that sad man at the garage where I was hiring a motor-car. It was a big —to me enormous—Chevrolet. When all the paper work was done, I timidly asked if he would be good enough to show me the controls. What controls? You got in and went, for God's sake. He seemed hardly to grasp what I meant when I confessed,

24

shamefacedly, that I was still, after 40 years, clutching and declutching and shifting gears. A man in a mechanic's overalls was summoned: and you would have thought, as he curtly and contemptuously told me to put the lever into 'drive', press that pedal and, God damn it, too, that he was having to teach me how to walk.

And I found out more about how to become an automan in thirty minutes of New York than in thirty years of Europe. Partly this was because New York and other American cities, and their connecting roads, are made, as is fitting, for automan, whereas ours were made for man and are only now and very awkwardly being made over. A man in a motor-car in London, Paris or Rome is only a man; he's rarely able to exceed for long the natural speed of his species, say 4 m.p.h., yet on the other hand there is almost nowhere he can stop. Thus, his car is revealed as a toy become a nuisance, and himself as absurd. But automan in New York whizzes up the even-numbered avenues and down the odd-numbered, east on the even-numbered streets and west on the odd-numbered. He may leave the machine-half of himself at the kerbside as freely as a footborne man in London or Lisbon may stand still on the pavement; more freely, for automan will never be charged with loitering. And this is because the authorities of the automan state naturally understand that respect is owed to the whole of every law-abiding citizen and not only to the organic half of him; and that it would be as unreasonable to consider the original, basic man apart from his mechanical symbiotic partner in automanhood as to consider a man apart from his legs.

Automan comes into his own on the parkways and turnpikes, for the use of which he pays heavy tolls without regard to the taxes his human half has already paid. But automan knows that he is a new and superior species and he pays, with contempt for the services man is obliged to do him. That is his pride, as it is his pride to keep the automanly laws like the one which keeps him moving at 60 m.p.h., no more and rarely less, and reading, at suitable intervals, *Speedsters Lose Licences*, as it might be *Sinners Lose Souls*.

It is understandable that we foreigners were a little alarmed by the automan we had confided ourselves to. This was not our George, nice, kind, human George. Not that he was less nice, less kind. Only, he became a Device. Here is the analogue I made: when, for the first time, I drove an automatic motor-car in New York traffic, I was made horribly uneasy each time there was a stop because I had no clutch to throw out, no gear to put into neutral; I could hardly believe that, nevertheless, the machine would remain still. Because George did not drive deliberately consciously, did not make one rational decision after another any more than did the automatic clutch somewhere under his feet, we, like apes in the presence of man's powers, were afraid.

It was on the return journey that I, at the wheel despite George's most understandable reluctance, discovered the compensation of being a mere man. We went down the fast lane at a nice steady 85. It was a sin, it was, if you like, a breach of trust and an ill return for hospitality. But I must be forgiven, it was perhaps my last revolt against the rising and soon to be dominant autohuman race. Not even those *Sinners Lose Souls* threats could shake me, for not all the might of Uncle Sam could take my English licence away.

Expatriates

The frontier area of West Bengal swarms with Tibetan refugees. Most of them, having spent the money they got by selling their little bits of jewellery on food, now live on charity, or die of starvation. There are a few families which remind me of the German and Austrian Jews of the thirties who saw what was coming well ahead of the event, got out with some capital and all their skills, and prospered in Britain. But even before the era of the refugees, West Bengal fashions and looks were influenced by Tibetan ways. The traffic is far from being one-way. After a day's walking and botanising in the hills above Kalimpong, we went for drinks—millet beer—and the Tibetan version of *canapés*, with a Tibetan family established and prosperous here since the Forties; they are people concerned with the exploitation of the Tibetan arts, especially dancing, as one means of enabling their fellow countrymen or a few of them to make a living. In short, a Far Eastern version of the commonest by-product of 20th century political lunacy and ineptitude—an attempt to recreate the old country in a new one and, if possible, make it pay. All the same I couldn't fail to notice that the eldest son of the house, aged 18, would, considering his sartorial style and his hair-do, have been at home in juvenile London, in pop society. Presently, as he watched us, with sardonic eye, suck millet beet through bamboo tubes (he prefers Coca Cola himself), he indicated a handsome Japanese record-player and asked if we'd like some music. Eastern music says nothing to me but naturally I said yes. The record which he put on was *Sergeant Pepper's Lonely Hearts Club Band*. And I wasn't all that surprised: after all, the Monkees had blared at us from half a dozen loudspeakers in the bazaar quarter of Djakarta; and the Beatles had been popular, as taped music in Rio's working-class cafés; and the sentimentalities of 'When I'm sixty-four . . .' had afflicted our ears from Chinese shops in Singapore. For centuries philosophers have been seeking a universal culture for mankind: boys, you're home and dry. And it's England that's done it again.

The Rich are different

'It's an utterly lovely place to live, isn't it?' 'Oh, very', I said but perhaps I didn't sound reassuring enough because the lady, my fellow guest, pushed her face nearer, insisting with her slightly frightened eyes on my paying more tribute than that, 'I'm afraid everyone must envy us', she said, 'I'm sure', I said, and she looked away towards the sea, 'Lovely, lovely . . .' 'Out of this world', I said.

We were sitting on the paved terrace of our host's villa. The paving was black marble squares alternated with squares of ceramic tessellation, and the terrace overhung a garden of great trees and irrigated lawns. The warm wind off the sea, carrying the scent of mandavilla and jasmine, was making us sweat gently. Twenty kilometres away up the coast the lights of the city made a saffron and rose glow in the sky. Nearer, the lights of a smaller town, 1,000 feet and six kilometres below us, were like fallen stars against the night-blue darkness of the sea. The lights of fishing boats and those of the villages higher up the mountain, suspended in darkness, gave me the feeling of being miraculously floating between two immense voids. The soft light we talked and drank by came from the open drawing-room of the house behind us and from the flood-lit fountain of the big comma-shaped swimming-pool where three of the younger guests were playing an improvised game of water-polo and laughing. I was eavesdropping the conversation of the two women who sat in the arbour of golden bougainvillea just out of sight behind my right shoulder. The one with the Dutch, or maybe German, accent was saying: '. . . they both came, the man as well as his wife, not 25, either of them, begged on their knees for the job, well, they all know we're easy employers. *Ma jere*, for three weeks they succeed to hide the truth. Four children, stuffed, like *dol mades farcies* in that hovel next to Beppo's with her mother to look after them, but Fritzi said in no time they'll be in and out of the house and tormenting poor Qwanyin, and Siamese are so sensitive . . .'

The light reflected from the dancing, musical fountain lit the heavy, down-drawn face of a fat man who waddled in front of me to join them, saying as he went, with a kind of ponderous eagerness: '*Und* another thing, Mrs Abelson, so a child falls and cuts its knee, the old woman sends another of the litter running up shouting and crying catastrophe, you know these people, so the mother quits her cooking and rushes down like the child was dying, and so then where's our dinner, and perhaps we have guests, *nicht wahr*? So, they had to go.' His wife said: 'Fritz was so good. He told them for me. Me, I'm soft'. The one they called Mrs Abelson said: 'If you're in gold it's no time to be soft. Silver, they said, but I wouldn't listen. It's being a romantic, there's something about gold. Did you hear Julia had to get rid of old Carmen? So sad, after 14 years, but 74 and arthritis in the hands, always dropping trays . . .'

A servant took away my glass and replaced it with another huge whisky on the rocks. Somebody said that in winter when the air was clear you could see Africa, and my first interlocutor said: 'Lovely, lovely . . .' and 'I hope you're not too hungry, Mr Hyams. Although we're not Spaniards we keep Spanish hours. I expect we'll dine at 11; when I first came from England it took time to get used to . . .'

We: the community of owners of the score of villas on the estate, with that climate, that view, like gardens, swimming pools, fountains, all under the benevolent shadow of the *Caudillo*. My English lady went on, again insistently drawing my attention to the magical night: 'And you realise that I pay no income tax, not a penny, not to anyone.' I said I did know it; I could hardly help it—it was the first thing they told you, told you with a kind of little sly, sniggering look, an indescribable version of salaciousness as if they were deliciously breaking the last sexual tabu. I said, mock innocent: 'But surely, as a Spanish citizen . . .' and she interrupted: 'Oh, no, of course we keep our

British passports, or Dutch, you know, or whatever we happen to be.'

From the gloaming on the far side of the Italian marble table which was the centrepiece of the terrace, a plummy but barking voice, an, as it were, regimental voice, said: 'My chap says Wilson's going to devalue again. Says Franco won't follow suit this time, trying to persuade me to accept residential status and get out of British holdings . . .' and he went on to describe the financial operation which was to save him from Harold; and my mind became a blank as a defence against the tedium, the black tedium of the kind of small, crafty technicalities I'd had too much of all that afternoon. Because the Frenchman I'd been invited to meet (publisher, propagandist? tycoon? moral rearmer? I never made him out) had opened his proposition touching the translation and editing of a whole series of pamphlets, (sub-leftist? sub-fascist? sub-Catholic Action? I did not read enough to discover), with the statement that 'they' ('we') had a lot of Swiss money and he could arrange for my fees to be paid into a numbered account at a Swiss bank.

The regimental voice had finished its exposition and my lady said: 'My man says the same, I mean, about devaluation again; there's nothing Wilson won't do . . .' And to me: 'When do you think it will be?' 'I don't,' I said, 'I don't think it will be.' 'Oh, but my advisers . . .' Sowing with joyful irresponsibility, the seeds of doubt-induced, greed-fed insomnia, I said with the utmost decision that their 'sources' could hardly be as good as mine. Tall girls in pyjama suits, with theatrically perfect tans and long, golden hair moved in and out of the circle of gentle light from the open-sided drawing-room. Someone had put *Sergeant Pepper* on the record-player.

The tall Englishman whose cypress-girt hacienda had been pointed out to me joined our circle with the information that he'd been taking a sauna, in time to hear the English lady's question and my answer. Had we, he said, heard the new one about Harold? We had not, 'All that sittin' about, y' know. Late sessions, crises keepin' him at his desk. Got a nasty case of piles. Some of his friends—well, accomplices, he has no friends—kept urging him to see a doctor. Promised he would, but Harold can't keep a promise even to himself. Left it too late for treatment . . .' The Moroccan lady in silk robes, on my right, said: 'Please . . . piles? *C'est quoi ça?*' '*Les haemorrhoids,*' I said. '*Ah, le pauvre . . . Justement, mon oncle, le frère de ma mère . . .*' The raconteur raised his voice: 'decided the only thing was to do a transplant. The first, well, ladies present, call it anus transplant in medical history . . .' Nobody obliged with a cue and the Moroccan lady said: '*C'est curieux, je n'ai rien vu dans le Figaro . . .*' The raconteur said: 'Three days later, the arse . . . the anus rejected Harold Wilson.' The other Englishman guffawed and the lady on my left tittered. I got up and walked to the balustrade and looked out over the littoral to the sea. The raconteur joined me presently, 'Beautiful, isn't it?,' waving his hand. 'Couldn't live anywhere else, now. Better than poor old England, eh?' and insistently, 'eh?' Inevitably, came that shameless, shameful boast, with the side-sliding, confiding little glance, 'and not a ha'penny income-tax do I pay.' And, quickly: 'This your first visit to Spain?' I said I'd been there in the Thirties and Fifties. 'You must see some big changes?' 'The same,' I said, 'as I've seen all over Europe, America, Russia. Even Britain. More people making things of more raw material equals more and more of more and more.' 'Not in Britain,' he said. 'Do you know what I'd be paying in tax if I still lived at home? Over £3,000 a year. They've driven me out of my own country. No, say what you like, Franco's done a grand job here.'

Next morning, up at the inn in the village where I was staying, the water stopped running while I was cleaning my teeth. At breakfast they said: 'It happens, señor. Fortunately there was enough to make your coffee. It is the *rancho de los extranjeros*, señor. They have put the river into pipes. You have seen their gardens?' It was not a complaint: simply a statement of the facts. No question that my acquaintance of the dinner party was right:

Franco has done a grand job; he has, at least, retaught the Spaniards that Spanish proverb whose wisdom they were bleeding and dying to repudiate when first I was in their country: with the rich and mighty, always a little patience.

Guides

Charles, our driver and guide in Ceylon, could be as young as fifty or as old as sixty. A Buddhist, he is devout. He chews betel nut but not in our presence although he carries the makings— leaf, lime and nut, in the glove compartment of the car. When we stand about in the heat he cools himself by gracefully fanning with the skirt of his white sarong. He has devised the simplest social system we have met with anywhere in the world; as we drive through the teeming central quarters of Colombo, the markets and slums, he says, 'Here live unworthy people.' A little later we are in a kind of garden suburb of handsome villas in well-kept gardens and we ask Charles what sort of people live there: 'Only worthy people'.

Gypsies in Ceylon

We look down from the balcony of our bedroom window in Kandy. In the street just below, on the sidewalk beside the parapet of the great formal lake, there is a family of itinerant musicians: they sit on a cloth spread on the cobbles. The man plays a kind of harmonica which his wife pumps by hand. A small boy beats both ends of a drum with his hands and sings a seven-note refrain over and over again in an almost incredibly powerful voice. His sister, a child between ten and twelve, plays a flat drum: domestic harmony.

. . . *in the Soviets*

We never found out the status of gypsies in the Soviet Union. The only ones we saw were a family crossing the Red Square in Moscow, all of them very shabby especially the children and this was particularly noticeable in a country where the children are dressed better than the adults. But when we enquired about them from one of our Intourist guides, she had a short attack of diplomatic deafness.

Travelling on a tourist coach in Yugoslavia from Dubrovnik to Radimilje we passed three gypsy families driving in the opposite direction, their flat carts with goats behind and children beside taking up most of the narrow road. Our coach pulled in and the driver shouted angrily at the leader who replied with a sort of weary courtesy but made no great effort to clear the road. The children came to the windows of the coach and begged, making the almost stylised classic gestures, the older girls showing their babies. Most of the mixed bunch of American, English and Italian passengers threw small coins down to them. This infuriated the already angry driver and the young man accompanying the tour, who was one of the state PUTNIK guides, became very cross indeed . . . These people are a disgrace to a socialist country, they have no loyalties to the state; they steal the peasants' hens, their crops, the clothes off the line; they are verminous and breed too much and despite Government antipathy they continue to live here; we are encouraging them with our charity and this is unfair to the peasants whose land they are defiling. We were abashed; one American said, 'Take it easy, boy'. The driver started the engine and the coach moved slowly forward, nudging the carts, children and goats into the side.

What interested us was that, right or wrong though our guide's arguments were, they were, in fact, the same arguments used against gypsies in the capitalist countries; his dislike was the dislike of the good bourgeois who sees a group of people who are neither buyers or sellers—non-contributors, in fact. In all our travels we never came across anyone quite as true-blue Conservative as a good Russian communist; but the Yugoslavs run them close.

Hotels in Russia

Staying in Soviet tourist hotels requires three things: patience, a sense of humour; and above all a copy of Maxim Gorki's *Through Russia*. You need the book to remind you that the disconcerting things have nothing to do with communism and everything to do with Russianism. If the waitresses (a section of Soviet womanhood whose over-full figures, piled-up hair-dos, vivid hair-dyes and make-up, make them look like old fashioned whores) ignore your hunger and all sit down for a snack of their own, doubtless it's socialism which very properly allows them to do it; but it's Russianism which prompts it. The Soviet ensures boiling water in the taps; but it's old Russia which involves you in an obscure and complex row between Intourist and the hotel management resulting in your bedroom being left uncleaned and beds unmade until four in the afternoon. The Soviet spirit provides the menu translated into English, French, German and Japanese; but the old Russia produces such translations as 'beef-tea with rusks' and, my own favourite Russian dish after borsch, 'sturgeon fried in spit'. Hotel servants never tout for, or even hang about for, tips. If they accept one it is without a trace of servility. And they work hard for long hours. Yet the old amateurishness remains, the room is never actually dirty yet contrives to remain not quite clean. Down on my knees looking for a mislaid shoe under the bed in a first-class hotel, I found the floor swept and garnished, but I also found a large cardboard box full of empty mineral-water bottles. It was still there when we left four days later. Somehow it was reassuring and I hope it's still there.

Mexico to Melbourne

Spend a day or two in and out of the Mexican Museum of Anthropology and you'll surely be using its restaurant; and realising once again how pleasant it is to be in a country where public eating places and other resorts of public service are really clean. Why are the people of British stock such messy eaters and drinkers, and the people who serve them so wanting in self-respect? The Mexico City contrast is very striking—tables spotless, floors continuously swept, waitresses and waiters in fresh, clean working clothes, trays wiped dry and polished, every drink served on a clean tissue. But the moment you set foot in New Zealand you are back home in the nastiest kind of pub—up to your ankles in cigarette ends and litter, bars awash with beer slops, and the drinks slammed down like an insult. The pubs in small Australian towns or villages are even worse, squalid as an English pub in an industrial slum. Melbourne pubs on the other hand are cleaner than ours and the serving staff much more polite. (I am not writing about the smart places where the standard is the usual international one.) Eating in Melbourne is very easy and very agreeable. Both city and suburbs are very rich in good Italian, French, Greek and Chinese restaurants, and the excellent, so-called *smörgåsbord* places. Cooking is good, portions enough for two European appetites, prices reasonable to very cheap, service quick and courteous. But then all Melbournians seem to have gentle manners—even the post-office clerks and the police. Maybe it's the plenty of good wine that does it. A Mediterranean climate; good, cheap wine; a yeast of South Europeans to leaven the mass of British stock, such is Melbourne; and if they can find a way of persuading the brightest of the young citizens from rushing off to London or New York at the first opportunity, surely Melbourne has the makings of a golden city? And yet I don't know: it could be that Australians, in the great coastal subtopia all but a handful of them live in, are too pleased with their pleasant selves and easy life to tolerate the disturbance, the challenge, the irritation which original talent introduces. Maybe they ban books, not because they might corrupt morally, but corrupt socially and philosophically. And yet, again, so gentle: an old, sick man in poor clothes fell flat on his face under our feet in a shopping street; in a moment he had been raised by kind hands, the bleeding from a head-wound staunched, had been offered his taxi fare home by one woman, helped into her smart little boutique by another so that he could rest and drink tea. In Rome they'd have walked round him; in Paris over him; in New York they'd have arrested him; and in London—in London I'm not sure.

Reception

The manner of your reception at an hotel is more important than, as it were, the matter. For a striking example: no reception clerk at an hotel was ever more welcoming, more smiling, more anxious to please than the one in Rio de Janeiro who, with clasped hands, implored us to keep our money and our other valuables in a private strong-box which he would allot to us and which we would be given the key of during our stay. There would, he said, be no extra charge. I asked more or less jokingly, if there were thieves among the servants. He said, 'All our servants are thieves, on occasion, senhor.'

It seemed to me extraordinary thing for an hotel management to admit, and I said so. The Brazilian shrugged and said in his admirable French—the language we had in common—'If we all know where we stand, we shall all know how to behave.'

Where the servants really all thieves? I don't know. They were good servants and pleasant people and with our valuables under lock and key we were free to seem to trust them. And in one way they benefited from the reception clerk's slander—or candour: we felt so guilty at having distrusted them that our tips, on departure, were lavish.

Man to Man

I pulled the car off the road and walked back towards the narrow irrigation channel to look for a wild flower whose flash of colour I'd seen as we passed. A bullock-cart loaded high with sugar-cane went slowly past. Beyond the culvert a lean man stood

naked but for a loin clout and headcloth, up to his thighs in the
water of a vast, shallow tank, and cast his fishing net in a movement of great beauty which ended with the net falling, a perfect
circle, on the water. On top of the parapet which protected the
culvert from the road a man lay sleeping in the noon sun; he too
was naked. On his forehead was painted a white V with its base
at the root of his nose and its tops hidden under his hair,
bisected vertically by a red stripe: that mark, as my expositor at
the temple of Sri Ekambaranathar had explained, made him an
adorer of Vishnu; those who adore Siva wear three horizontal
white stripes.

I stood and stared at the sleeping man and did my best to
make real the fact that we were of one species. Uneasily I
assured myself that the difference between us was simply one of
horse-power; I had command of more mechanical energy. The
man opened his eyes and for a time which seemed very long we
stared at each other: there was nothing I recognized in his eyes,
not even curiosity or resentment, and I suppose nothing he
knew in mine. Had I known Tamil or he English it would have
been the same. I knew from my morning in the temple among
the hundred million gods of the Hindus that he could not have
made me understand about the mark on his forehead or I him
about the pride in denial called humanism or stoicism. What we
did have in common divided us in every interpretation. I turned
away and watched the fisherman cast his net again; that gesture,
being an economic act, I could at least understand. If only for
that reason Marxism has a universal appeal, since the pang of
hunger is the same whatever the colour of the belly.

In the temple that morning the old man with the red teeth
and fleshless body—so pleasingly spare and hard after the
womanly fleshiness of those saffron-clad and stony-eyed
Buddhist clergy whom I'd met in Ceylon—expounded the
avatars of his manifold god. He showed me the god as fish, as
pig, as lion, as everything; other gods and goddesses and god-
animals—or perhaps they were all the same one—danced,

fought, helped men and women and cows to sow and reap, loved, sat at stool. In a sense I could have wished to be without his explanations, they required no gloss. Had I been left without the theology I could not have failed to find what I had in common with the creatures of the great sculptors who decorated the temples of Kancheepuram and Mahabalipuram between the 6th and 8th century under the Chola kings. Gods or men or beasts, these creatures done in bas relief, in the huge early mono-lithic carvings, or in the round, are vividly alive, elegant and beautiful with life being lived. I could have looked and looked for days if only the holy men with their involved nonsense would have left it alone. How they poison the well of life, the holy men, whatsoever gods they serve or pretend to serve. And after all it was not they, but princes or municipalities who, whether in South India, or Italy or England, paid the artists who beautified the temples. Yet despite the befogging theology which so nearly marred what my eyes had taken in and my heart rejoiced in, the sculptures of Kancheepuram and Mahabalipuram had left me with an exalting feeling of 'common humanity' until the moment when that Tamil with the Vishnu mark, on the culvert parapet, opened his eyes and looked at me. The gods were between us, an insurmountable barrier of nightmare fantasy.

Because I had to say something to the old devotee at Sri Ekambaranthar, it was the 'life' or perhaps the life-worship of his beloved bas reliefs that I talked so warmly about. He gave me his curiously sardonic, sideways, incomprehensible grin and said, perhaps only with intent to get a few rupees: 'The old kings were full of charity towards life. They were men of love. A king went out in his chariot to attend in person to the welfare of his people. Presently he came to a place where a long shoot of jasmine plant lay all across the road. Being unwilling to run over it, he got down from his chariot and moved it gently to the side of the road; then he took one of the poles of his chariot and erected it as a support for the jasmine. But he saw that the jasmine had not the strength to climb the pole. So he moved

39

his chariot onto the verge of the road and released the horses and laid the jasmine on his chariot and went about his work on foot.'

Prejudices

Correction of prejudices: in Venice the canals are fairly clean and don't stink; in Leiden they are foul and do stink. Very good French cooking is cheaper in Germany than in France. Levels of traffic noise are, in Holland, atrocious; in Belgium bad but bearable; in France abominable; in Austria low, excepting in Vienna where they render life miserable; in Germany and notably Berlin nearly as low as in New York. Worst noise offenders? Mopeds (Holland) and big trucks (France and Italy). Italy has improved in this respect. Most brutal and ill-tempered driving—Dutch; most skilful and good-tempered driving—Italian. Most careless driving—Belgian. As for the famous vicious driving of the Germans, I did not see an instance of it; Berliners have excellent road manners and so do the Munichers. The DDR police, encountered four times at frontiers and once for exceeding the speed limit, are polite, smart and cautiously friendly and, most heartening this, clearly so bored with the idiotic frontier checks and controls they have to submit one to that they openly scamp the work whether dealing with foreigners, or other Germans. Where the police have both arms and power the air becomes unbreathable. What a pity that communism, morally so superior to capitalism, has to be imposed by the most immoral of all forces—an armed and powerful police.

The Narrowed Mind

Travel may broaden the mind but it can certainly narrow it. If my mind was immensely broadened towards the Hindus, especially in southern India, it was narrowed, in at least equal measure, towards the Buddhists in Ceylon. I don't know when I've been more disappointed in any manifestation of human genius than in the Buddhist temples after I had seen half-a-dozen of them—two dating from the 13th and one from the 20th century. The latter is a remarkable example of *art nouveau* which in any case I detest. In the others which included the Temple of the Tooth in Kandy, the conventionally reclining statues of Buddha seemed to me not so much serene as quite lifeless and wanting in power, communicating nothing whatever, although I am not ignorant of the story and the feelings they should evoke. Shoddiness and *bon-dieuserie* are worse than in many Catholic churches. The priests, with their fleshy, womanly arms and shoulders, shaven heads and hostile, calculating eyes, are repulsive. In one temple an acolyte, having made flagrant homosexual advances to me and been repulsed, tried leching Mary; he also made a determined attempt, thwarted by Charles, our driver and guide and a devout Buddhist, to steal my miniature camera. At one temple a funeral was in progress at the graveyard across the valley separating the temple hill from the next hill; the officiating priest used a powered electronic amplifier and his address, lasting more than thirty minutes, sounded for all the world like one of Hitler's more hysterical outbursts.

Cricket in Australia

We were lucky to visit Australia in the off-season for Cricket. Neither of us know very much about the game and any experience we have of it is confined to local village matches where the finer points of the game give place to local patriotism.

Graham McInnes, in his evocative *Humping my Bluey*, gives an excellent account of the pernicious influence of cricket on human nature. He had been in Australia for 12 years, in fact, since he was eight. He was staying with friends when the English team arrived and because of his English birth his friends assumed that he would be a fervent supporter of the English team. In fact, he hoped that the Australians would win.

As it turned out it was an ill-omened year—the year of body-line bowling, and by the Third Test—the English had already won two—the atmosphere was tense, and the heart had gone out of McInnes's support for the English team. He and his friends heard the commentaries over the radio; heard the ugly scenes at the Adelaide grounds and the English victory was a bitter one for Graham McInnes. He went up to his room, convinced that his friends would never wish to see him again, and started to pack his suitcase. Whilst he was doing this his hostess came in and told him not to be a fool and he burst into tears. After this any pretence that he might have had to be English was dropped, and he and his friends all concentrated on hating the English and their new and vicious techniques.

All of which reminded us of an Australian doctor friend, who left Australia in the 1930s by way of a short-service commission in the Australian Navy; came to England where he took his doctorate and 'walked the wards'; served in the late war in the RAMC and when we knew him was a well-loved general practitioner in Chelsea.

Talking to him in the 1950s he said that the first time he realised that he was no longer Australian but British was the day when he found himself following the English team's performance in the Test Match, not the Australians'.

St Louis

St. Louis: the Mississippi waterfront and recalling whole passages of my second favourite novel, *Huckleberry Finn*. And then that magnificent and idiotic Gateway Arch: one minute you're sure it's engineering for engineering's sake like the Eiffel Tower (and why not); the next you're sure that the 630 foot stainless steel horseshoe upended beside the river is a mighty work of sculpture, a sweet, towering, pure curve against the pale blue of the sky, a shining glory swinging vertiginously backwards, remote above your cricked neck and reeling body and dazzled eyes fixing on clouds which are racing but seem still. And then there are the tall buildings in brick or stone the colour of old dried blood, blown-up Victorian Peabody Buildings piled appropriately heavenward. And then that wood-panelled bar and diner where the beef was respectable and they had a proper understanding of the superb red wines of Sonora and Napa, so very superior to 98 per cent of the over-priced imported ones. Yes, St. Louis is now my American city even though, back at the hotel, the lobby was crowded with stout, flabby men in funny hats, standing in inward-facing groups and yelling. Who were they, I asked the aged bell-boy (bell-boys in America are all so old and infirm now that pity makes you carry your own luggage and tip them just the same). Tigers, he said: God knows they didn't look like it. And that's a thing I've never been able to get guidance on—baseball. My work in St. Louis was interfered with and made more entertaining by this unsightly and tedious game, the match being between the St. Louis Cardinals and the Detroit Tigers. On TV screens in offices, laboratories, workshops, it distracted everyone's attention, and mourning over the Cardinals' defeat was universal and loud. It wasn't as if the people I was dealing with were businessmen; they had serious work to do. My only moment of enjoyment was when the colour went haywire and the little players on the screen had grass-green faces while the pitch was crimson. But this is the point I want clarified: do academics, professors, researchers, really care passionately which team wins? Or are they, like English politicians at a Cup Final, pretending to be partisan so as to appease the herd?

Books in Argentina

A poster in the post office of a small town in the province of Neuquen told me that the Argentine Post Office can teach at least one trick to our own money-hungry PMG—if only our booksellers would let him use it, which, of course, they would not. What the poster announced surprised me so much that I took the trouble to confirm its information: the Minister of State for Communications issues his own catalogue of books in print by Argentine writers. This is delivered free on request by the postman. You send the GPO an order and a money order for the book or books you want; and they are delivered, post free, to your house. Presumably the Ministry receives the bookseller's discount from the publisher and can pay for the service out of that. Ostensibly the idea is to encourage the reading of native writers and the growth of an Argentine literature; and to overcome the bookselling difficulties in a country where the rural and small town populations have no access to bookshops. Some ranchers and their workers may have a drive of as much as three hours to even the smallest kind of shops, and over atrocious dirt roads at that. The Argentine market for books is not large by our standards, but it is growing and the publisher can export to all other Spanish-speaking South American republics, and even to Spain; and literate Brazilians—a minority—often read Spanish. All the same Argentina's problem like that of every other formerly colonial country with an ethnically European population, is to hold the native talent against the pull of Europe. Those Argentine writers whose work is known outside their own country do not live in the Americas but in Paris or maybe Rome, just as Australian actors come to London. No 'new' country can hold the local talent against the Euro-megapolitan magnet unless it can itself offer an art-and-letters megapolis. But one force working in Argentina's favour is her soft currency; it is relatively easy for a New Zealand genius to escape, if he wants to, to London, Paris or New York; financially, it's very difficult for an Argentine.

How to live in Australia

Films, books and loose talk, often the loose talk of the Australians themselves, have left a majority of the English with an entirely false idea of what Australia is like. We think of it as a country of the Frontier, of sheep, cattle and wheat farmers, fruit-growers and prospectors, tough, hard men living an open-air life. In point of fact, however—and this is a truth which must begin to filter through to us soon—the Australians are the

most urban people, Australia the most highly urbanized
country in the world. Or, rather, at least by our standards,
suburbanized. Towns—I except Sydney—tend to have no
detectable centre, and sprawl over an enormous area of land.
Of Australia's twelve million people, I was told as if it were
something to be proud of and maybe it is, eleven and a half
million live in half a dozen towns, and the rest of the country
is more or less empty.

We had seen the way people live in those towns; much the
same as they do here or in America, only food is a lot cheaper,
so is wine, and you are apt to be ordered out of a bar if you have
not got a tie and jacket on even when it is much too hot to be
wearing either: that is the measure of Australia's towniness.
The cities are pleasant enough, certainly: Melbourne, for
instance, despite its enormous population, never feels as
crowded as our cities do because everyone is allowed more
room; after all, room is something they have a great deal of.
Sydney is one of the most beautiful cities in the world; in a
totally different way so is Canberra, although every Australian
I talked to sneered heavily when the place was mentioned. But
what we wanted to discover was how an Australian farmer
lived his life, what his home was like; the kind of farmer we
were interested in was the kind equivalent to our own medium
to large farmers; that is an agricultural technician with a degree
in farming, not a peasant. Not that there are any peasants in
Australia; that is one of the things which is wrong with a
country which, on the whole, has much less wrong with it than
most places. A couple of million peasants of the kind who can
get a living off ten acres while steadily improving the quality of
the land is something Australia could do with. However, that's
beside the point. We found our farmer, or rather he found us;
it was a party—Australians give more parties per month than
we give per year—and all we knew about him at first was that
he talked very well indeed about Australian painters, including
one who was an 'Abo'—Australian for Aborigine.

Party acquaintances are liable to become friends in Australia in a way they very rarely do here; the Europeans, including the English, are as a rule grimly determined to keep strangers, and especially foreign strangers, out of their homes; the Australians have none of this rather rebarbative attitude and at the end of that party we found ourselves invited to spend a week, two if we liked, or as long as we could manage anyway, at our new friend's sheep ranch, only they don't call them ranches or farms but stations.

To get there, a few days later, we went by road, in a hired car: now, here, another aspect of the Australian's urbanization; the people seem positively frightened of the country, the outback. We were strongly advised not to try to drive all the way; it would be a thousand miles of boredom; if the car broke down, then what should we do? It was hot; we should probably get heat-stroke or die of thirst. If we had to stay overnight in a small town on our route, we should find it primitive and very uncomfortable; and so on. Well, as we had quite recently made a four days drive across Argentina, including the *pampa seca*, from Buenos Aires to the Andes; and as I have been driving in four out of the five continents since my mid-teens, we decided to ignore this advice, and go. We found that there was a perfectly satisfactory road; that, having virtually no other traffic on it once we were away from the city, it was a motorist's paradise. As for being boring, the countryside, utterly different from anything either of us had ever seen anywhere in the world, was fascinating in its very flatness, in its curious subfusc colouring, its mirages, its groups of eucalyptus trees. At last we began to see why Australian painters paint the way they do. It was hot, certainly, but not as hot as motoring in, for example, Ceylon or southern India. As for the small town we stopped in overnight, its hotel was a most entertaining mixture of Victorian English and 'Frontier' American in, say, the 'nineties of the last century. It had baths for ladies and separate baths for gentlemen, in cubicles in a sort of annexe. The food was of the kind

47

you can only get here nowadays by going to a very bad hotel in Scotland, or maybe Ireland. And the only adventure was when we were asked to move the car to a place where abos from a neighbouring colony, going 'walk-about', could not be tempted to ransack it for anything they could find; the police object to people putting temptation in their way.

Our friend's house was a bungalow, built mostly of wood painted white, very spacious, with large, light rooms. One of the legends about outback Australians is that they do not care twopence about the graces of life, about art or letters, or even about the comfort of having good furniture, carpets, well-considered decorative schemes. The two farm houses which we visited, this one and another some miles away, were furnished at the very worst most pleasantly, with the kind of taste which does not entail vast expense; and, at the best, in some of the rooms, with half a dozen pieces, from early to mid-Victorian, which were admirable. Australians have become very conscious of their 'antiques': old houses are preserved, at least in some places, although in others the very real grace of Victorian building in the towns, with the typical cast-iron work, balconies and iron columns, is being recklessly swept away. (Sydney, notably, but Melbourne also, has some of the prettiest Victorian streets still left anywhere in the world.) Their antique furniture is not antique enough, by our standard, and one sees objects treasured which you would have a job to sell even in the Portobello Road; but these things are valuable in a land where people are only now beginning to realise that as well having a tremendous, sometimes even rather frightening, future, they do have a past, even if it is rather a short one.

Our friend's house had, on one side, what we should call the farmyard, with outbuildings to store tools and machines, a pleasing wooden cottage for the farm foreman, a poultry yard, and, by the way, the enclosure where our hostess kept her two tame baby kangaroos, both of them orphans of farming accidents; or possibly as a result of the dams being shot. One has to

be very cautious, nowadays, in pronouncing any species of
animal to be safe from extinction, but it does seem as if the
kangaroos are standing up remarkably well, and we saw for
ourselves the kind of damage which they can do even to a very
large field of corn, stripping away acres in a night. On the other
three sides of the house was garden; and it amazed me to see
what could be done in a region of severe drought, in the way of
garden-making and maintenance; and to see, also, how much of
their very precious water ration our friends were willing to
devote to keeping their garden green and blooming in a landscape which looked, to our unaccustomed eyes, as if it had been
blasted by fire from heaven, as indeed, in a way, it had; for the
sun that season had been merciless, and it was very painful to
see, when our host drove us about the farm during the next
several days, (it was about a quarter million acres I think), the
wretched sheep keeling over and dying before our eyes: not of
thirst, of course, they were watered, but for the want of grass
to eat.

The garden was one of enclosures made of clipped evergreen
hedges, of lawns, rather rough but no amount of watering,
even if there had been water to do it, could have made fine
lawns by our standards; of flower-beds and shrubberies and
some fine old fruit trees. One of the things which fascinated
me about Australian gardens in general, and about this particular
one also, was the way in which familiar designs, familiar layouts,
familiar dispositions of plants, are carried out in strange materials:
of course, Australian gardeners use most of our own garden
plants as well, and are as passionately fond of roses as so many
English gardeners are. But you see such lovely things as callis-
temons, melaleucas, leptospermums (from New Zealand) and
many other unfamiliar kinds. There will be orange trees or
lemon trees where we should have apples or cherries, and
often, the much more unfamiliar tropical fruits. That farm-
house garden was particularly beautiful at dusk, fragrant and
cool after the watering which I was allowed to help with. If

you sit long into the dusk on an Australian garden veranda, with a lamp for reading, you are apt to be slightly taken aback by the size of some of their night moths; half a dozen, of a species which is about nine inches from wing tip to wing tip, drove us indoors.

It would be foolhardy to generalize from just two country houses; but one thing was very striking, that Australians seem to be interested in and to collect their own painters, and to be much more knowledgeable about painting than one would have expected of a people who, in another mood, take a perverse pleasure in mocking at the claims of art. In England art is international; if there is anything specifically English about modern British painting I have quite failed to see it. But Australian painting is as Australian as Italian Renaissance painting was specifically Italian; and there are Australian farmers who look at it, enjoy it, understand it and talk about it. I found that impressive.

French Illusions

Three old illusions about the world of books in France: one, that the publishing structure is more literary and less a matter of flogging a commodity than ours; two, that Frenchmen are readier to read the new, difficult experimental writers than we are; three, that French readers still judge for themselves what they should read. As to the first illusion, there are maybe five real publishers still left, people who may use the methods of the big scale purveyors of more or less useful printed matter, but who do it in order to finance the publishing of literature. For the rest, in France as in the United States, Germany and Britain, it is bankers' business, accountants' business and has the same criteria as any other international commodity merchandizing operation. At a guess, American capital is stronger in France than in Britain when it comes to the publishing trade. The bright young publisher of the 'fifties, risking his bit of capital in backing his taste for literature, his intelligence and his flair, has become the hard working and well-paid servant of his banker, trying very hard to avoid any sort of risk.

Then there is the business about the French and new writing: the new writers have not been helped by the reading public, but by the remainder of the real, loyal publishers; and, oddly enough, by the film makers. I confess that I was taken aback at some of the figures I heard quoted: the publisher who takes on the first, brilliant novel of, let's say, a latter-day Robbe-Grillet, can expect to sell eight hundred copies of the book. At a guess— well, it's something a little better than a guess—a new work by one of the new novelists with a name, a reputation, perhaps a film to his credit, may find five thousand buyers—that is if there are plenty of long reviews and maybe a TV appearance. You hear talk in book circles—at all levels—about the awful situation in America and Germany where book buying means buying that month's best seller and nothing else; and where nobody actually reads even the book they do buy. You'd think you were among the Pure. The fact is that a book awarded the Goncourt Prize, or one of the other big prizes, may well sell a quarter of a million, be it good, indifferent or downright bad; and that just like everyone else, the French read the moment's fashionable book.

Where French publishers maybe do a better job than ours is in making foreign work available. The list of a firm like Gallimard for example may include as many as eighty translations a year, and of those only about 25 to 35 per cent from the major languages; and that despite the fact that the French are very reluctant to read translations—books which were considerable successes here, Svetlana's letters for example, were not so in

France. The chances of a translation making money for the publisher are smaller there even than here. Listen to people who get their living from books, in Paris, talking about foreign writers, translation: it will be borne in on you that for 'English' you must understand 'American'; excepting in theatre, the French are much less interested in our writers than in modern American writers. I was given, for what it is worth, one explanation: American writing is not very foreign to any culture, at least in the west; English writing is still obsessed with what is so English that it is almost untranslatable.

One enormous difference between their publishers and ours: at nine I telephoned a director of a big publishing firm to make an appointment for that evening; he was in his office and took the call himself; I called to pick him up at his office—at seventhirty; heads of departments and most of the staff were just leaving.

Washed Notre-Dame

Washed, like St. Paul's, churches like Saint Germain l'Auxerrois, but above all Notre-Dame, reveal a brilliant new beauty. I suddenly realised the sheer joyousness of twelfth to fourteenth century gothic. What exquisite pleasure there must have been for the builders in making those great windows, in fretting that façade, in so contriving that the bare minimum of stone shaped and contained the maximum of light and space. That the noblest gothic soars away from earth instead of pressing comfortably down on it, as a Greek temple does, is a commonplace; but the truth of it becomes a thousand times more striking, more moving, when the building has been restored to its original lightness of tone matching lightness of form. This is startlingly revealed in Notre-Dame at the moment, October 1969, because the cleaning job is only half finished, so that parts of the cathedral are still black and grey with the dirt of centuries. The dark parts seem now to anchor the creamy golden cleaned parts to the earth, to hamper them; they do not soar, but crouch. For how long did Notre-Dame and the great temples of the north European age of faith give full expression to the intention of the artists who made them and who, of course, used the colour of the stone they shaped, as well as form, in their compositions? In other words, for how long did they remain clean? That darkening by dirt, so cherished by those who mistake buildings for etchings, must have been progressive; and so, also, therefore, the building's loss of power to work upon the spirit as the builders intended. Contemplating the cleaned Notre-Dame, emerging like a revelation in the autumn sunshine, I saw why Spengler compared gothic with western, non-Euclidean, mathematics: in both cases there is a glorious emancipation from the burden of mass. The masons of Notre-Dame made stone weigh nothing; then dirty Time, blackening what should be light, weighed the great fabric down; now the cleaners restore the missing element of the old builders' weight-eliminating art. What a shame, from the point of view of those who believe that the loss of faith was a loss indeed, that the restored revelation of the gothic cathedrals comes too late.

A Penthouse in Buenos Aires

One of the most pleasing, surprising and cleverly designed homes which we saw in the course of our travels was on the twenty-sixth floor of a tall building in Buenos Aires; what is more it had the makings of a very charming garden; I say 'the makings' because it was all very new, and although it had been planted, the shrubs and flowers had not yet had time to grow. The art of roof gardening has been carried further in the cities of the Americas, North and South, than it has been with us; their greatest difficulty is that of high winds, often winds of gale force. In some of the very high roof gardens which we saw in, for example, New York, windshields were of some kind of pierced fabric; apparently experience has shown that it is better to check a wind than to try to stop it dead. But in our Buenos Aires friends' penthouse the problem had been solved in one place by a massive wall which had the added advantage that french windows into the dining-room, could be opened even in windy weather, and elsewhere with fine mesh grilles.

Had I lived in that flat, I do not believe that I should ever have got any work done at all; from all the windows the views over that lovely city are stupendous; and however restful views over open country may be, there can be no doubt that a really wide and extensive panorama of a great modern city is far more consistently absorbing than any view of mountains or downs or fields can be.

The dining-room of this penthouse was originally two medium-sized bedrooms. Our friends the Drysdales knocked down a partition wall to make one very large room with an open plan arrangement; and as they wanted to make the room seem even larger, and to be as light as possible, they had the whole of one wall covered with a single gigantic mirror, which created the illusion that the room, a big one in any case, was twice as large as its actual size. This room opens through french windows onto the principal terrace of the roof garden; it is furnished with a number of good pieces from England and France, mixed with modern pieces, the armchairs and sofas for example.

When the Drysdales took the flat it had five tiny bedrooms and an equally small kitchen with one of those *va-et-vien* doors which are guaranteed to break someone's nose sooner or later.

By removing partitions and by internal remodelling all this was changed, and on the floor above the living-room they now have a very large bedroom and a bathroom again with magnificent views over the city; and an adjoining room which is both dressing-room and study, the walls completely lined with books which compose a remarkable collection of, as it were, *Argentiana*—history, botany, ornithology, zoology. A thing which we noticed repeatedly in both Buenos Aires and elsewhere in Argentina was that Argentines of English, Scottish or Scandinavian descent are, on the whole, much more interested in such things as the topography, flora and fauna of their country than Argentines of Latin descent, the original Spaniards, or the French and Italians.

From every window we looked through there were those lovely views over the city as far as the mouth of the La Plata river. Having very little idea or experience of the enormous size of South American rivers, I made a complete fool of myself by asking whether, on a clear day, it was possible to see across the river to Montevideo, the capital of Uruguay: I was told gently that no, this was never possible, the distance in question being two hundred miles.

My principal interest was in the roof garden, or rather terrace garden, for it is not quite literally on the roof. The sitting-out space is decoratively paved with crazy paving in soft coloured stones, and round this the flower beds are built up of stone 'bricks' to give the surfaces of these low walls a very pleasing texture. The problem of drainage was a considerable one, but in the end it was solved simply enough by draining the water from the flower beds into a central sump under the paving, above which is a small grating to drain the paving itself —Buenos Aires has a fairly high rainfall in winter—and the sump drains into the main drainage system of the building.

Straight lines were avoided in the shape of this charming little garden poised three hundred feet or so above the city streets, for the clever use of curves makes the area seem to be much larger than it really is. The flower beds were filled with a sterile soil with a very high proportion of peat; this has reduced weeding to a minimum up to now; but I would guess that as time goes on, weeding will be almost as much of a chore as in an ordinary garden owing to the half dozen or so species of birds who frequent it and who are, of course, great seed carriers.

I have already mentioned the problem of wind, and the plants for a very high roof garden always have to be chosen with care. So it is useless to plant wind-sensitive species. Here the Drysdales have made use of small-leaved, low, dense bushes such as the dwarf rhododendrons and dwarf hebes. To obtain a third dimension, however, they were using small conifers, junipers and cypresses; some of the cypress plants did not look as happy as the junipers. Surprisingly, at least to me, for Buenos Aires can be cold in winter, and at that altitude frost cannot be discounted entirely, some dracaenas were doing perfectly well.

The plants being used to cover the blank walls were only just starting to grow, and I noticed that hard wood plants which were being trained to the walls were standing up to the conditions much better than the true scandent or climbing plants—twiners like *Lapageria rosea* (a native of the extreme west of Argentina) and plants which cling by means of tendrils, like the Passion Flower vines. I think that where there is so much wind at certain seasons, wall plants without rigid stems were bound to be knocked about a good deal unless very thoroughly tied in. Mrs Drysdale asked my advice: it was to clothe the walls either with a thin screen of cypress clipped to give it density, or box treated in the same way, to make the whole into a green room as it were; or else to try a selection of the English variegated ivies, alternating silver and gold cultivars, with plain greens. However, since she wanted her wall plants to have flowers, she decided to persist with various flowering vines until quite convinced that they would not survive.

Although alpine shrubs are the principal plant material of this roof garden, Mrs Drysdale also makes use of many alpine bulb species—crocus species, miniature daffodils, tulip species and scyllas, very sensibly avoiding the much bigger garden cultivars which would have been quite out of proportion with the dwarf shrubs, and for that matter with the scale of the garden itself. One suggestion I made was that although the kitchen of the flat does not open onto the garden, it would be well worth having a decorative stone or lead tank planted with culinary herbs.

Pleasant though it was in daylight, this twenty-sixth storey garden was a place of real enchantment at night when one could sit there for hours, enjoying the scent of a *Mandevilla suaveolens* flowering on one of the walls, and following the lines and curves, avenues and stars of differently coloured light, with the eye, to the foreshortened night horizon; and watching the lights come and go in the tall buildings across the city. It is true that for a night townscape, no city can compare with New York; but the air of New York is so dirty that one can sit outside in comfort only on the very highest roofs; the tenth-floor flat which we are allowed to use when in that city has to be permanently sealed against masses of half-burnt paper from inefficient incinerators which drift, like black snow, onto the roof garden. Buenos Aires lives up to its name, however, and one could sit in the Drysdales' garden breathing the mild, clean air off the La Plata, and wondering at the new beauty which electricity has created in our cities.

Napoleon's Face

Have the French at last, despite fire-eating historians and gangster-adoring biographers, come round to Anatole France's view of Bonaparte, I mean his Trinco in *Penguin Island*? There

seemed to me very little heart in the bicentenary Napoleon
exhibition in the Grand Palais; and although we went on a
Sunday, visitors were not numerous. Maybe the organisers
should have taken a trip to Moscow and a look at the Lenin
Museum; for the Russians really do understand how to worship
a fellow citizen who put them through the mill. Of course, there
were some pretty things to see; neo-classical goldsmith's work
for example; and a remarkable tapestry by Bissardon and Bony
of Lyon, its vivid bouquets of flowers so exquisitely well done
that they could have been used as accurate botanical illustrations,
or by an horticultural historian to identify cultivars. One
singular comparison with the Lenin Museum: no Trotsky in
Moscow; no Talleyrand, or for that matter Fouquet, at the
Grand Palais. Come to think of it there is another likeness; the
set-piece paintings are atrocious, and in much the same manner,
grandiloquent and wooden. I've never seen so many rocking
horses in one place together. Can there be any significance in the
fact that the two best paintings are not of Napoleon but of his
mama? In Gerard's portrait of Madame Mère you can see all
the sons; the Greuze (1800), shows her elegant, sad, sceptical—
one remembers that grim *Pourvu que ça dure*—and, despite the
painter's gentle manner, firm.

Good or bad, the portraits of the emperor are fascinating;
properly arranged, they make a sort of rake's progress; as the
power grows, the face spoils. In an early profile head and
shoulders by A. J. Gros, showing the long chin and mean mouth,
the utter humourlessness probably essential to a big-scale killer
is already apparent. Still, in all the early representations there is
a sort of young Byron quality, even in a Vann-Bree which might
have been done from a waxwork, and in Appiani's *First Consul*
which is oddly, and surely unintentionally, villainous. Remorse-
lessly, with the years, the Mussolini face pushes through the
skin; it's very evident in P.R. Vigneron's (1809) jowly and sulky
full face, but already immanent in Appiani's 1805 portrait of
Napoleon as King of Italy. In a Gerard portrait loaned by Mrs

Bachmann-Naegli something even more sinister has been revealed: from behind the Napoleon-Mussolini mask glares a baser countenance—Al Capone's. The final and clear emergence of the Great Gangster is depicted, however, in the Horace Vernet portrait loaned by the London National Gallery.

By the way, why is it one never hears a word of Monsieur Père? Didn't all those Bonapartes have a human father? Madame Mère does look a bit like the sort of woman some of the Olympians used to fall for.

Brown in Argentina

Ricardo called for us at the hotel; I had not yet seen enough of Buenos Aires; it is one of the most agreeable cities I know, with a sort of Parisian smartness in its shops and manners which is very pleasing to a dyed-in-the-wool European like myself. On the other hand, the prospect of a drive across the sub-continent and up into the Andes was an exciting one. The car looked like something between a gigantic jeep and one of the cars used by staff officers in forward areas in war time. It had enormous ground clearance, two spare wheels, a coil of rope, a great many tools and a large can of water. We were to take turns at driving but I insisted on Ricardo taking the first stint, so that I could look about me at B.A. possibly for the last time in my life; I never count on being able to get back to places, however much I have liked them.

Much as I should like to, I am not going to describe that drive; I want to write about the way some people live in Argentina and the sort of houses and gardens they have. It is a temptation, though; there were places where there was no road at all and we had to fight our way through the deep sand of a track; places where the land beside the road was of low cactus plants as far as we could see, with their gorgeous flowers which seem to be made of silk; there was our first sight of the great fast-running, flightless bird the *Rhea* which the Argentinos call an ostrich and which looks like one; our first llama.

Ricardo had said that we would stay at houses belonging to his family each night on our way across the country: for he belonged, although you would never have known it from his quiet manners and modest tastes, to a rather grand family, with ramifications all over Argentina and beyond. Two of the houses we were to stay in were no longer in continuous use. Various branches of the family used them for holidays, or, as we were to do, for over-night stops during journeys from one side of Argentina to the other. 'Even for that', Ricardo explained, 'they are not so much used as they once were, now that my brothers fly themselves from one *rancho* to another in their own aeroplanes.'

I do not know that I have ever been more surprised by anything I have ever seen as by the house we stopped at the first night: we had come through scores of miles of short grass country, level plain with a few stands of eucalyptus trees here and there, an occasional broad, low house, a rare horseman wrapped dramatically in a cloak and wearing a broad-brimmed hat, half a dozen lorries, two or three 'ostriches', a couple of llamas. Then there had been sand and cactus country, where on every roadside post there perched a hawk. (For the benefit of bird-watcher readers, I had never seen so many raptor birds as in Argentina, just as I have never elsewhere seen as many simply beautiful birds as we did in Australia.) We were very hot and, from the dust of sand roads, indescribably dirty. Then, quite suddenly, we began to climb, the air became cooler and damper, there was lush green grass beside the road, clumps and plantations of trees. We stopped for a drink from our flasks, ours of warm whisky and water, Ricardo's of one of the cola

drinks for which he had an inexplicable passion, perhaps his
only fault.

Presently we saw a spectacle I could not have believed
possible in that alien landscape: a large English country house,
superbly sited on the flank of a green hill, flanked by cedars
and set among sweeping lawns defined by exquisitely placed
plantations of hardwood and conifer, including the glorious
araucarias which are among the splendours of Argentina.

I was still gaping with astonishment when Ricardo turned the
car into a beautifully 'serpentine' drive, drove slowly along it
between magnificent woods, and pulled up at an enormous
Palladian portico. Ricardo explained that his grandfather,
founder of the family fortunes, had built the house; he said we
should find it sad; it had been built by a patriarch whose sons
and daughters had children to fill it—but how was he to know
what would happen to the world?—those children now had fewer
children . . . 'But,' he said, 'we shall try to make you comfortable.' And he uttered that phrase with which Spaniards, rather
than Argentinos, welcome you to their homes: 'This is your
house.'

I did not even go inside to wash at once; I was too fascinated
by this translation of a great English style to so remote and
alien a place; and in any case it would, we were told, take time
to 'animate' the ponderous hot water system to supply the
bathrooms put in, with the water closets, by a Staffordshire
firm in about 1909; and as for food, Argentinos, like Spaniards,
eat their evening meal as near midnight as possible, being
reluctant to go to bed in case something happens while they are
asleep. I went out into the park—for that is what it was, an
18th century landscape park.

Supposing that I had been asked to 'place' a house like that,
but in an English landscape, and to attribute the landscape
garden to a particular artist, I should have said that both house
and grounds were by Capability Brown, before the time when
his style as an architect had been lightened by the influence of

Robert Adam, and more effectively by his young friend and
protégé, Henry Holland; for the house has a certain heaviness
of the kind which a little marred his style: but there were his
cedars, framing the house, there his vast sweeps of lawn; there
his 'clumps' of trees so placed as gently to emphasise the
undulations of the land. The serpentine drive was his, too; and
above all the serpentine lake, now badly choked with reed and
water-lily. But then I was shaken in this impossible attribution:
one lawn surrounded a pond so formal, so rectangular, in its
dressed stone basin, so backed by tall, thin trees planted in ranks
like soldiers on parade, so decorated with a superb pair of
bronze cranes from China—beyond question they were
Chinese work for the cranes were standing on tortoises—that
the ghost of Brown faded and the ghost of Le Nôtre took its
place.

Inside, the house had nothing whatever of Capability Brown
about it; it was, barring the colossal open fireplace in the dining
room in which a huge fire of cedar wood had been lit, for the
evening was cold, the purest Victorian. Our bedroom was
panelled in some yellow wood which had been heavily varnished
and then 'combed' with a false grain. The bedsteads were
brass, the window curtains of Nottingham lace . . . After a bath
—the bath taps were brobdingnagian—and dressing in front of
a fragrant wood fire, I went out to fetch something from the car
and returned through the back entrance: that back façade of the
house shook me again; the clumsy Victorian portico, the
ridiculous little Franco-Scottish turrets beside the gables—it
was suddenly the sort of house which belongs in a Sherlock
Holmes story.

Ricardo's other house, the one of our second night, could
hardly have been more different. By then we were in foothill
country; and although the house stood not among alps and
streams, as it were, but on a plateau with, again, that low growth
of silken-flowered cactus among which Ricardo's brothers had
bulldozed their airstrip, still, it was a mountain house, a long,

low bungalow with a chalet-type roof although there could never be snow there. In front of it was a pretty little alpine garden, and a great bank of, surprisingly, heather. Inside the house there was almost as much light as outside, a great rugged stone fireplace, one immense, studio-like room with the other, very much lesser rooms opening from it. On tables, shelves, window-sills were the pieces of a collection of prehistoric stone tools, weapons and implements dug up on the property and in its neighbourhood, and which any museum curator would have given an eye for. Immediately behind one open showcase full of such stuff was the big radio which Ricardo's brother used for getting meteorological forecasts before he set out for B.A., or another of the family properties.

What about servants? The house was run—cleaned, warmed, cooked for, laundered—by a woman who might have been any-thing between thirty and fifty, five feet tall, slight, pretty until she opened her mouth and revealed its toothlessness. It is surprising, the amount of work that Spanish Americans can get out of a servant weighing perhaps eighty pounds, maybe eighty-five; especially if, like this one, she had seven children and, being a Chilean who had slipped illegally across the border, she had no rights. Of course, she had a husband; he kept her pregnant, pretended to work in the garden which was actually cultivated by a small and perhaps idiot boy whom he clearly had some hold over, drank the best bottles out of the cellar of wines from the province of Mendoza which the family maintained there, just in case, but had to be respected because he was male and arrogant.

There, too, there was good Victorian furniture from the whole warehouses of the solid, indestructible stuff which grandfather had imported. But the plumbing was of lighter gauge, not so massive but more elegant, and bore an Italian name. The Chilean drunk had remained on his feet long enough to make his report to Ricardo with a proper air of respect, and to get the electricity generator working, so that we ate our dinner of

63

pasta, and what was probably rabbit, by the mixed, flickering lights of uncertain electric power and a fire of eucalyptus logs; they drew deep red gleams from the polished wood sideboard which would have been in place in Mr Barrett's dining-room in Wimpole Street.

The Gift of Tongues

Despite the use of slang which remains briefly fashionable, the French respect their language in a way we do not respect ours: I mean the spoken tongue. Few English people take pleasure in deliberately making the fullest possible use of their speech. We are satisfied if we manage to convey our meaning more or less, often less; and our speech is nerveless, sloppy, frequently mutilated. The difference between the two peoples in this respect is certainly not due to differences between the two languages; they favour English which is richer in words, especially in words conveying shades of meaning; compare, for length, the English–French with the French–English parts of any good dictionary. And in any case both the Irish and the Welsh can show us what can be done with spoken English, using a larger vocabulary and so placing their words as to exploit all the flexibility, colour and depth of which the English tongue is capable, and so conveying a feeling or communicating a thought more completely than do our own feeble locutions. And our failure to use our language is not confined to the under-educated; the linguistic clumsiness of most persons of consequence talking or being interviewed on television or radio is lamentable, by comparison with that of most equivalent Frenchmen in the same circumstances.

But the difference is most striking at the public bar and workmen's bistro level: the French working man involved in an argument with his mates uses a much larger vocabulary, pronounces more of his words clearly, makes greater use of voice harmonics to convey significance; and, more remarkably, exploits the structure of his language to get the most out of it. Our own people miss one of the major daily pleasures in their inability to play with the language, and at the same time failing to communicate as completely as they might. I do not pretend to know whether this is a matter of education or perhaps of temperament; but it is certainly not a new thing: Taine noticed it a century ago. It seems to me a pity even if we ignore the aesthetic aspect; for if, as I believe, subtlety of thinking depends on and is proportional to degree of ease of access to locutions, poverty of language impairs quality of thought. Perhaps much more use of drama in the teaching of English would help.

Comrades on Holiday

Say 'Russia' or 'Soviets' and you see snow; and shades of grey down to black, people bundled against the cold till they look like bears; the relief of golden onion-cupolas against a frozen sky. Actually, quite a lot of the Union is Mediterranean and quite a lot sub-tropical, and those are the parts they flock to for holidays, if they can. Vronsky's and Anna's stolen holiday sequences in the new *Anna Karenina* film we saw in Kiev, incidentally, the best from-a-novel film I've ever seen, were shot with the Yalta to Livadia coast standing-in for Italy: it's as lovely a coast as you could find anywhere in the Mediterranean. Another holiday coast, south-west and north-east of Odessa, is tamer but beautiful. Most Russian holiday-makers reach it by train. But the favourite way if you have the time—they get from 3 to 4 weeks holiday with pay—is by miniature cruise-liner from Kiev, down the Dnieper by Kanev, Cherkassi and Kherson. On board they spend their time eating, listening to music, dancing; at Kherson you change to a big 300 seater hydrofoil which hurtles you to Odessa in two hours. Or you can fly there: Russians use aeroplanes casually, the way we use buses; within the Union, and for the natives, they're cheap, fast and by our standards uncomfortable. There's no bar, light refreshments consist of a glass of soda-water, and you're apt to have a couple of active children crawling over you. No dressiness: Russians travel a thousand miles dressed as for a stroll in the neighbourhood park.

There are five ways for holiday-makers (native, not foreign), to stay. You can stay at your trade union or professional union hostel or rest house. Not only the manual workers' unions have them. For instance, the Russian equivalent of the Authors' Society has a big one near the beaches at Odessa; they're very cheap, very unluxurious without being uncomfortable, and would hardly suit you if you liked privacy; a sort of Butlin, communal holiday, and that's for the majority. If your doctor gives you a certificate, and it may be for no more than over-fatigue, you can stay free or nearly so at one of the vast, innumerable holiday clinics which, white and deeply embowered in dark trees, star all the holiday coasts for miles. Some are brand-new, many more are being built; a few are old palaces, converted—like the Livadia palace where the Yalta conference was held, or the Alupka further along the coast, with its magnificent 'English' park. Both reached from Yalta by a gloriously sited corniche road overlooking the beaches. Then, a few, a very few natives with extra room let holiday lodgings: about a rouble (10/-) a day per head. If you are an Honoured Worker (dancers, actors and authors high on this list) you may have been able to afford a *dacha* of your own, or you may, like one acquaintance of mine, have inherited one: wood, two rooms, a big covered veranda, and a small garden; it may be by the sea or river or lake. Finally, hotels: disregarding the for-foreigners-only Intourist luxury class accommodation (bed, breakfast and a car and guide for 3 hours a day—£8.10.0 a head), these, old or new, have all the usual fittings, but sub-European standard. Fairly clean, slightly shabby, relatively dear for foreigners, cheaper for natives.

Beach life is beach life: what interests in the Soviet resorts is not how different it is but how much the same. Standards, in auxiliary amenities, are nearer to, say Viareggio than, for instance, Long Island on the one hand, Juan-les-Pins on the other. Beaches near Yalta and Odessa were not so crowded in May that you couldn't put a foot between the prone sunbathing bodies. Plenty of swimmers, though the water was cold and does not warm up until July. Soviet holidays are staggered over a longer period than ours but they said it got very crowded in July and August; said it, too, with pleasure. Crowding is what Russians, like Italians and Americans, like. They love the human race as we do not. Pneumatic animals, mattresses, boats; and underwater swimming gear are all to be had, but at a fabulous price, by our standards; still, somebody buys the things and when judging the cost of play, as when judging the cost of living in general, one has to bear in mind one very important fact: extremely low rents; most Soviet citizens have more left to spend after paying the landlord-State.

There are swimming and various kinds of pedalling toys on hire for the kids. But it is quite likely that the Russian holiday-maker may not have children with him: certainly, there are rather fewer on the beaches than one sees in, say, Italy or England. Soviet children have a three month summer holiday, from the beginning of June to the end of August. We watched the Last Bell ceremony in Minsk and Kiev—the children parading through the streets wearing the little white forage caps of holiday liberty, led by a military band loaned by the local garrison commander. Don't start thinking of the *Hitlerjugend*; the children were all over the road, laughing and dancing, and couldn't have been less soldierly. An amusing end-of-term tradition in Odessa: with a week of exams to come, the teenagers take over the square at the top of the famous Potemkin stairway, where the statue of, of all people, the émigré Duc de Richelieu stands, to the exclusion of adults, and exchange rumours about what the exam questions are to be. Tolerated as foreigners with an outlandish disregard for local custom, we watched a cheered teenager crown Richelieu with his little brother's liberty cap. As one might have expected of a member of that family, the duke continued to look dignified. However, the point is that there are holiday camps to which you can send your children, although the children are likely to spend at least a month of their long vacation with their parents. As in all intensely conservative societies—Communist and Catholic societies are fascinatingly alike in this as in so much else—The Family is given much weight. A Soviet child's life is in the hands (very good hands, if the look of the children is anything to go by) of the maternal State; but it has a private sector. As one young woman told me: 'I take my little boy to nursery school every morning. If I do not come for him by seven in the evening, he will be put to bed. But then, he cries'. Still, one must be sensible, a young couple I talked to had a joint income of 250 roubles a month: their two children spent two out of three months holiday at a holiday camp-summer school where they got four meals a day, expert care, medical attention, rambles, excursions and organised games or sports, and some light holiday tuition such as botanising expeditions; this cost the parents 5 roubles a head per child per month.

At all events, fewer kids on the beaches, but not so few as to make them bleak. But, on the whole, the universal beach habits —bikinis are not so prudish as in America, not so exiguous as in South French resorts; dark glasses, but fewer and flimsier; plastic nose-guards to prevent sunburn of the nose. A singularity: Russians enjoy sun-bathing, yet you see more ladies with sunshades in Soviet resorts than anywhere else in the world today; and another—there is, on the whole, less disregard for decent manners in the flaunting of old, fat, flabby flesh than in a lot of Western resorts. It's nice to find self-respect in the old again: we saw another instance of it when a man of perhaps seventy-five entered a restaurant with his old wife, who looked like Krupskaya as she would have been at seventy, took one look and one listen at the East German tourists living it up very noisily, and with beautiful dignity turned and marched out. Was this what they'd fought the Revolution and Civil War for?

Up off the beaches, a difference appears and suddenly, in the want of physical elegance, this is the Soviet Union, and like a down-sexed, sovietised, semi-silenced Long Island—but only sartorially. There is the same indifference to the quality of materials, the same aesthetically unfortunate illusion that a man's a man for a' that. Of course, there are exceptional girls, even a few youths who look more than merely tidy; but by and large nobody's clothes fit or tell you anything about the wearer, or brighten the street. The strolling holiday crowds are staid. Off the beach, no bikinis or any other form of semi-nudity. And no snogging in public places, not even in the dark velvet nights in the pretty gardens which are half Yalta, with their arbour-sheltered seats and small winding paths among well-kept shrubberies. The lights they switch on a little after twilight are no help to lovers—incredibly powerful things on tall steel poles, shedding floods of hard, penetrating, white glare. It's not really that, though: sex is bad form, the Soviet youth is brought up modest, almost prudish. But there's a pleasant enough atmosphere of easy, quiet contentment, and a kind of moderate gaiety, in the resorts, a relief after the grim humour of Moscow, but then so was even Kiev. The usual antithesis between the northern and southern temperament, and partly a matter of climate, no doubt.

Drinking plays a smaller part in their holiday pleasures than in ours. And not because it is difficult or, apart from spirits, very dear, although it isn't cheap either. The very mildly alcoholic *kvass*—if it is alcoholic at all—seems to take the place of coke, for children as well as grown-ups drink it from the small trailer-tankers from which it's sold by the glass in the streets. In the Southern resorts, Georgian and Russian or Ukrainian wines are sold in the same way. Those with a taste and the money for the better—in fact superb—heavy dessert wines of Georgia do their drinking in the quite pleasant wine shops where you can buy either by the bottle, or, standing, by the glass: the glass is a tumbler, and the wine costs from as low as 16 kopeks, to as high as 45 kopeks, a glass. Vodka and 'koniak' are both very good and very dear. In Yalta and Odessa we saw a few drunks, not spirit drinkers, but real winos, Australian style, and equally quarrelsome. People in the streets and wine-shops pretend they aren't there. I don't mean they're a social problem; only a mild nuisance, probably on a blind after a year's hard work. In the Soviets, as elsewhere, the real alcoholism problem is in the north, and in the industrial centres, not in the pleasure and health resorts. At meals we observed two ways of drinking: our own, that is with a light wine—their light wines are good, reds hard to get, both far too dear for a wine-growing country. And another way—large quantities of beer accompanied by periodical nips of vodka or brandy. Fruit juices are usually grape or apple or something that tastes like syrup of figs; tomato juice, excellent. Most people seem to drink mineral water, which is also good. And then there's tea with meals, as much the custom as in Ireland or Australia, but milkless. Not that there seems to be any shortage of milk: children and adults alike buy it and drink it by the bottle. My own gastronomic discovery, and the only one I'm ever likely to make: at luncheon on an aeroplane between Yalta and Tashkent I was served a large bowl of brown fluid which I assumed to be *consommé*: heavily salted and peppered, I found it most refreshing, though it was tea.

Most holiday-makers seem to eat at cafeterias, other than those getting their meals at their hostels or rest homes. The food is cheap and very nasty indeed; and the cafeterias, like those at the lower social levels in Britain, are rather squalid. There are some big, modern, fancy-lit ones, with hard working dance bands. Hotel restaurant meals are much dearer. I suppose the food isn't bad and there's plenty of it. I'm a bad judge since I am not an enthusiastic eater at the best of times. The holiday makers liked it but didn't much care what it was like; for example, nobody ever complained at hot dishes being, what they always are by the time the waitress has got them to you—say half an hour—from the kitchen, cold. Soups are good, also sturgeon dishes. Meat is awful, but then if you're English or French you're spoilt for meat elsewhere; there simply isn't good meat anywhere else. Russian chicken is tough but full of flavour, a welcome change from our blotting-paper broilers. Eggs are eggier, too. Very few people ate caviar and for a good reason: like us, they couldn't afford it; travellers' tales of cheap caviar should be ignored. We saw a lot of native 'champagne' drunk, at about 35/- a bottle, but mostly by East German tourists who travel in large parties, do themselves very well, and become rather noisy. Most people seem to smoke, including policemen on duty; cigarettes are very cheap, even the excellent imported Bulgarian ones.

The dancing, in the bigger cafés, in hotel restaurants where the guests let their food get even colder in their enthusiasm for it, and (Yalta) in a big open air dance hall or, rather dance park, is very much what you can see anywhere. Most people just shuffle about a bit; but there's plenty of jive and twist to slightly old music, but then dance music everywhere seems to have a way of casting back a year or two, or five. Nothing later than the Twist, nothing like improvisation on the Shake, unless that was what we saw in Tashkent. I'm coming to that, and certainly the dancing can get very lively indeed and Russians really love it. Dancing manners are good, even rather formal at first. If a man wants to ask your girl friend for a dance he'll be careful to ask you, with a slight bow, first. If you object, that's that. Not that you do object: he's probably taller than you and anyway as wide as a door. At the big outside places in Yalta, under orange lights and with competing bands, one of which seemed to be amateur, the going was rough; maybe they were doing the Shake with modifications. But Tashkent was the place to see the Soviet citizen dancing. They had the loudest, fastest, hardest-working band I've ever suffered from; not a moment's respite. Foreign girl tourists were constantly being left, looking a bit silly, twisting, while their Uzbek partners went cavorting off in a wild, stamping, leaping dance with much wild and graceful arm and hand work, across the floor, accompanied by Scottish-sounding whoops, and by a band which obligingly changed from recognizable jazz of some sort into unrecognizable and much wilder Uzbek strains. I restrained my friend from offering to teach these splendid pupils *Knees Up Mother Brown*: they were already doing extraordinary things to, of all tunes, *The Lambeth Walk*.

Plenty of other entertainments but no special, light, or pop summer theatre. Lermontov and Chekov at Yalta, which has the little Chekov Theatre near the Chekov house museum (fascinating). Films at the same level, in cinemas which are bleak, rather dear, meant for taking The Film seriously. If there is any pop art in the Soviet, it's imported. In Odessa, they have the lovely Opera House, an architectural gem, with opera, ballet, concerts with foreign artists. The place has other theatres. Music is far more a part of ordinary people's lives than with us, and an extremely high proportion of children apparently learn to play an instrument. We talked with a visiting French singer: what did she think of the hotel? *Infecte*. The food? *Infecte*. The internal travelling (she was on a tour)? *Infecte*. The Soviet audience? *Une merveille*. Then there are the little pleasures which, in holiday places, depend, especially for children, on small traders, street stalls, booths, ice-cream cars. Some, at least, are there, presumably the only 'private sector' of the economy, and you could buy sweets, fruit, flowers, books, even, oddly enough, postage stamps; above all ice cream. I was told, and by an American and therefore an expert, that Soviet ice cream was really something. Certainly, everyone eats it all the time. I tried it: it tasted like any other ice cream to me; only warmer.

A House on a Frontier

From Calcutta we flew north, in a small aeroplane to the military airport at Badogra. From there our friend's house was an hour's drive, climbing all the way through teak forest. As this country on the Sikkim frontier was threatened by China— Chinese troops had been across the border not so long since— the whole region was under military government and we had to obtain a special permit to stay near Kalimpong. At the Airport a car was waiting for us, its driver, a small, broad, wiry man with a nut-brown face much wrinkled by smiling; he was a Sherpa, and he drove with as much caution as if we had been doing our climbing on foot instead of on wheels, which was a relief as it happened, for we were constantly meeting hazards; the worst of these were convoys of army vehicles, driven flat out by magnificent looking men in turbans. The road was wet, for a sort of scotch mist was seeping down through the treetops, so that fast avoiding action was apt to put us in the ditch, and as this road followed an endless series of tight hairpin bends the whole way we were glad of a driver who crept round them hugging the near side of the tarmac. Then there were the monkeys which seemed to prefer the nice open space of the road to play in, to the teak forest beside the road, with its carpet of big, tough dead leaves and its canopy of deep green. However, at least in their case it was the monkeys and not ourselves who had to take avoiding action. Then there were the long files of women and boys making their way from the tangerine orchards which we could just see through the trees, off the road to the left, to some loading point. They carried their enormous loads of fruit in very long, poke-shaped baskets secured to their backs by a band round the forehead, and the strain of humping that load up hill seemed to distract their attention from approaching traffic.

The house when we reached it was outside and high above the town of Kalimpong, a good half an hour's walk from it. It stood in a large garden and was approached by a conventional curving drive of beautifully maintained gravel between perfect lawns. As the house was being lent to us during our friend's absence in Calcutta, we were greeted by servants: five of them were standing on the doorstep, to smile shyly, bow, seize our luggage. They seemed to be of several different ethnic groups, which was likely enough because this part of India has had a very mixed population—Bengali, Sherpa, Sikkimese, and a great many Tibetans. For when the Chinese seized Tibet, many people fled the country and took refuge across the borders, and Kalimpong had a considerable Tibetan population, some of whom had settled down to work in business of one sort or another, and were prospering—our car, for example, was from a Tibetan hire firm; others had to be supported by charity.

We explored the house, conducted by the cook because although he would not be the servant waiting on us, he had more English than the house man or any of the others; the gardeners spoke none at all. We had a large sitting-room, with a view of the Himalayas; it was furnished in very conventional English style of the late 'twenties and early 'thirties, and had, necessary in late autumn, a good fire of logs burning in the open hearth. Then a dining-room, furnished again with English mahogany although the carpet and hangings were Indian; it opened into the kitchen by way of a hatch; at meals we were served by two servants, very deftly and silently; and although they withdrew the moment a course was served, they invariably reappeared at precisely the right moment to clear that course and serve the next.

Upstairs there were a number of bedrooms; ours was a large one, very simply furnished with twin beds, dressing table, armchairs, all English style. The floor of polished teak was only partly covered with Indian, Tibetan and Persian rugs. It was apt to be cold because we did not ask for a fire in the room—the supply of firewood was limited and difficult and the local electricity supply was not up to operating electric radiators. Our very first awakening in that room, after our first night in the house, was a great deal earlier than we expected: I think it was about five-thirty in the morning that we were roused by repeated knocking on the door, and an urgent summons, 'Sahib, Sahib, you can see The Mountain . . .' The Mountain, in Kalimpong, is Kanchenjunga, 28,146 feet and the third highest mountain in the world. We were out of bed in a moment, and at our window: the spectacle was one of the most beautiful I have ever seen, and extraordinarily moving; very far away, but towering above a line of pure crystalline white against a sky of pale blue, the snows of Kanchenjunga were dyed the most exquisite shade of shell pink by the rising sun. We watched it, shivering but indifferent to the cold, until a great curtain of dramatic cloud, drawn upwards from the remote valleys, obscured the mountain. Thereafter, whenever the sacred peak— for it is held in religious reverence—was visible at dawn, we were called by that knocking and that urgent cry, '. . . you can see the Mountain'.

Just as the house was a pleasant English country house, so the garden too was very English. There were fine lawns defined by flower-beds planted with herbaceous perennials, almost all of them perfectly familiar. There was a bank terraced as a rock garden in which, again, nearly all the plants were familiar, although some of the rarer primulas and the meconopses, being native to the Himalayas, were more flourishing than they would have been in England. There were HT, Floribunda and climbing roses, among them one which one would not usually see in an English garden, the lovely Macartney Rose, *Rosa bracteata.* There were shrubberies of rhododendrons and camellias, very much at home in the moist coolness of those mountains. Only some of the garden's trees were unfamiliar and some of them I never did identify. One horticultural singularity did puzzle me a good deal; not only in that garden but in all the gardens of the neighbourhood there were flourishing groups of poinsettias, their scarlet bracts waving everywhere like bright flags on the tall, rather gaunt stems. Nothing remarkable in that, they had obviously been planted by gardeners who happened to like them. But there was so much poinsettia also in hedges, coppices, all over the place, that I came to the conclusion it must be naturalised, rather remarkable for a native Mexican plant.

I should have enjoyed doing a little gardening in that English garden perched up in the foothills of the Himalayas; we had been travelling for nearly six months and there is no better way of coming down to earth than handling the stuff. But the moment I stooped to pull out a weed, one of the silent, smiling gardeners, who seemed to have a force of unofficial auxiliaries in the shape of two pretty young women, was at my side, taking the weed under my very nose; in the end I gave up for fear that my weeding might be interpreted as a reproach.

The house and garden were so pleasant, run with such silent, calm smoothness that the atmosphere was wonderful for working; and the garden, in the warmth of the day, so delightful, that we were almost reluctant to leave for the walk down to Kalimpong. But when we did make that walk we were very well rewarded: there was, in Kalimpong, a garden even more attractive, and much more richly planted, than 'ours'; it was, indeed, one of the most successful gardens we have seen anywhere in the world. It had been made and was maintained by a very remarkable gardener, the half English half Tibetan, Mrs Victoria Williams, who with her sisters owned and ran the charming little Himalaya Hotel. Central to this garden was a terrace of fine lawn with a superlative view over the densely wooded hills and the distant mountains; the garden was on three levels, steeply terraced on the hill-side, so that from this lawn one looked down on plantations of magnificent hardwood and coniferous trees, and shrubberies rich with rare rhodo-dendrons, mostly of the Himalayan species although there were some of the exquisite Chinese kinds; with camellias grown to an enormous size; and with a great many flowering shrubs which I had very rarely seen in any garden. The garden was also remarkable for superlative bush roses, climbing roses, honey-suckles, clematis in variety; and for lilies, although we were too late to see many of them in flower. But what could keep me busy for hours was going slowly about a garden which, over a long period of years, had been added to by a really great plantswoman, looking for the hundreds of kinds of rare small plants from the mountains which one could find there, gone half-wild, remark-able little primulas, all sorts of violets, alpines familiar and unfamiliar including a great many saxifrages.

Every evening whether we had been down to visit a family of Tibetans with whom we had made friends, or to spend an hour in Mrs Williams' garden; or had stayed at home, in the sun of our own garden, or working indoors, the cook would make his appearance with his notebook, suggest the meals for the next day and discuss them with us, and then get us to sign the account for his purchases which we always did without question.

There would be that dawn call on the mornings when Kanchenjunga was to be seen; then another call at eight, 'Sahib, Sahib, bath . . .' The bathroom was a conventional one, but all the water was carried up in great copper vessels from the kitchen boiler. And then another quiet day at the desk and in the garden, not allowed even to 'do' the flowers with which the gardeners filled the house. If you are a writer who is thinking of emigrating, I recommend Kalimpong; in all the world I never found a more agreeable place to work in, or one where the conditions for working in peace were so good.

The Smell of Durian

It is possible to stay in Djakarta, city of arrogant little Generals and miserable beggars, as luxuriously as anywhere else in the world, at a price which I estimate at about twenty pounds per day per head. But we had, for the work we had gone there to do, to go up country, first to Bogor where Sukarno lived under a kind of house arrest in a palace which is, in fact, a great English country house in the Palladian style, set in a lush green deer park of fine lawns and magnificent trees which might have been landscaped by Humphry Repton; and then to Tjibodas in the high hills still further inland. We had been told that there was a hotel in Bogor and that we could get a car which would take us there in a couple of hours. Our driver was a university student of engineering, earning his living by driving a taxi; he spoke fairly good English and told us how his father had been a rich man in Sumatra, how he and his mother and brothers had migrated to Java when his father died, and how his mother had bought him the car with what remained of the family fortune.

The drive, about fifty miles, was fascinating, for the road presented, all the way, a very lively scene. The country, which is of course hot but has an enormously high rainfall, is unbelievably lush and fertile; rice fields alternate with woods and fruit plantations. Peasants wearing very becoming straw or grass hats about a yard in diameter, and shoving or hauling barrows which they moved always at a trot, were bringing durian fruits, very neatly made up into triangular packs of six with pandanus leaves; and jak-fruit similiarly packed, and piling them beside the road for transport into the market at Djakarta. The stench was atrocious; durian is said to be delicious and very nourishing, and I am willing to believe it, but as it smells exactly like a badly neglected dustbin, I never got near enough to one of these enormous fruits to try it.

From outside, the hotel did not look too bad, in fact the long, curved façade was quite impressive and as Sukarno's prison palace was almost opposite, the outlook was pleasant enough. But that was façade only, as we realised a few minutes later, when a swarm of red-tarbush'd porters had carried in our luggage and then, in a long trotting file, led us to our quarters. They consisted of a decaying bungalow with a veranda furnished with cane chairs and a table, all very wet and dirty. Inside was a bedroom with two iron beds, a rickety wardrobe, a chest and two flimsy, straw seated chairs. The floor, which was either of beaten earth or some kind of composition, was uneven and the lower parts of it were not damp, they were practically puddles; it was very dirty indeed. Opening out of this room, which was swarming with mosquitoes, was the bathroom. This was a sort of dressing-room with a brick floor and leprous brick walls; in one corner was a lavatory, but there was no means of flushing it; in another was a tall cement tank full of brown water of sinister aspect; you bathed by standing naked beside this and pouring water over yourself with a kind of saucepan. The smell of drains, or rather the absence of drains, was worse than all the durian in the world.

We had two days of this; it was not pleasant, with the temperature in the high eighties and low nineties; it was only on the third day that our friend the Director of the great Indonesian Biological Institute, asked us casually where, by the way, we were staying. When we told him, he was horrified; he had been under the impression that we were commuting to and from Djakarta. And it was thus that we were offered and lived for a time which was all too short in one of the pleasantest temporary homes we have had. The Guest House in the *Hortus Bogoriensis* or, in Indonesian, the Kebun Raya, one of the world's most beautiful and spectacular gardens, covering several hundred acres.

This garden, a botanical one, of course, was founded by the Dutch in the nineteenth century, and of the Far Eastern gardens I have seen only Peradeniya in Ceylon can compare with it. Although it was Dutch, and is now superlatively well maintained by the Indonesians, it owes something to England: Raffles was personally interested in Botanic Gardens, founded two, and set his mark on the design of very many Far Eastern gardens. So the shape of the Kebun Raya is that of a great English landscape garden, with fine lakes, great sweeps of lawn, an undulating topography, and tree planting which is almost in the manner of some of our greatest English landscape garden artists of the late 18th and early 19th centuries. But the plants, trees, shrubs, perennials, the lot, are all tropical and consequently far more spectacular than we are used to. The result of this marriage of English garden style, tropical plant material, and Dutch and Indonesian horticultural expertise, is breathtakingly lovely. And in the midst of this beauty we had a small and very pretty Dutch house, solidly built of brick and tiled, to ourselves. True, a part of it was occupied by one of the under-gardeners and his wife and mother-in-law, who added to their minute wages by catering for and serving the Garden's occasional guests, in this case ourselves. But Indonesians are so quiet, so slight and deft, and so gentle (excepting when they are fighting mad, when they can be very formidable indeed), that these people could not have been more unobtrusive.

Our living room and dining-room was furnished with nondescript Dutch furniture all of it very comfortable. The big casement windows framed one of the loveliest scenes I have ever had before my eyes for any length of time: one of the great lawns, falling away in a gentle slope to the largest of the lakes; the lake was brilliant with tropical water lilies and backed by a great bank of flowering shrubs, hibiscus, frangipani, and I no longer remember what; beyond these were towering trees, many of them flowering trees, and even taller Royal Palms and other palms.

The bedroom was as simple as the living-room—two beds, a wardrobe, a dressing table, a floor of polished teak, all exquisitely clean. From its windows we should have had a view of the mountains up country from Bogor, but they are perpetually covered with heavy masses of grey, dark-blue, and purple cloud, for ever on the move, but very rarely breaking. The rain-fall in those hills is about ten times England's mean annual precipitation. But never have I seen so many shades of green as there were in the foreground, the greens of leaves and grasses; and rarely so many different textures of foliage.

Our bathroom was on the same principle as that of the hotel, but as different as chalk from cheese, for the tank holding the bath water was tiled in white, the lavatory had a proper drain and even a proper flushing device although that did not work; still, a large bucket of water stood perpetually beside it, and although I never filled it or saw anyone refill it, it was kept always full. Everything was scrupulously clean, and even the water in the tank was so clear that you could see to the bottom and confirm for yourself that no disagreeable creatures were lurking in the depths, as one suspected they must have been at the hotel. As the tank held a very large quantity of water, it was 'standing' water, and so took on the temperature of the air. So there was no shock in pouring it over yourself even when the outside temperature was up near one hundred; that water was soft and mild as milk.

We visited three of the houses of people—scientists and administrators—connected with the Kebun Raya. All were furnished in the European styles; one rather luxuriously, with heavy Dutch and German furniture, dozens of fine Oriental rugs of various countries, and some good pictures. Another, bungalow style and more recently built, was furnished with 'modern' furniture; and everything, decorations, clothes, pictures, the record player, the manners of the two children, the food and the conversation suggested the home of a European family in a highish income bracket and with intellectual leanings.

Like all Indonesian houses built on European lines, ours had a long veranda: I do not know that I have ever begun days more pleasantly than sitting on that veranda, eating papaya with lime juice, and the tiny eggs which Indonesian chickens produce, drinking bitter black coffee, and looking not at a newspaper full of international robbery, arson, rape and slaughter, but at the flaming colours of cannas, and the subtler ones of water lilies, against that magnificent background of towering trees and palms; and mighty thunderheads of cloud in strange contrast with the blazing sunshine of the garden itself.

Suffering for Fun

Driving recently through the Welsh Valleys, I said to Mary that the whole district would soon become derelict as more and more pits were closed, then who would live in all the endless rows of houses? She suggested that the whole area should be geared to receive American tourists and envisaged a tour in which they would be invited to live like an old-time Welsh miner; in a miner's cottage, suitably modernised, of course, and meals to be taken at a conveniently sited canteen/restaurant. I thought this funny and rather shocking. Now I read[1] that in fact US tourists are paying £160 per head for a three week holiday to learn first hand how poor people live; and that the

[1] *Evening Standard.* Oct. 30. 1969.

people of Cinderella in West Virginia will benefit from this mixture of rubber-necks and genuine social workers who wish to see a real poor soybean-eating community. True, although Cinderella is an abandoned coal-mining region, it has none of Welsh cottage accommodation. On the other hand, the chances of seeing two Welshmen settle a row by duelling with six-shooters in the streets—I gather this happens in Cinderella—are small.

Why stop at that, though? What about tours to Calcutta with gutter accommodation to learn what it's like to die of starvation; or to a Bantustan to find out what apartheid feels like from the wrong end? Maybe our travel agents could sell Americans the idea of accommodation on a bench on the Thames embankment, with old newspapers for blankets thrown-in free of charge.

Phoning Round the World

At Colombo we put Victoria—fourteen and coolly self-confident —on the aeroplane to Melbourne and some hours later flew to Madras. It was the following night that we began to worry: it was a long journey for a child on her own; her sister was expecting her, but suppose she managed to miss her at the airport . . . we saw her, a small, small figure lost in that vast continent; or suppose—well, any of the nonsense anxiety suggests. At seven that evening we put in our telephone call to Melbourne. We began the almost unbearable torment of just waiting; at hourly intervals we got some relief by asking the operator what had happened to our call. It was in hand; it seemed that everyone in southern India was trying to call Australia; her patience and her English were equally admirable;

and we were reminded of a passage in André Marling's *Spanish Fare* (Cassell. 1963):

'Telephone operators need to be exceptionally long-suffering. Their nerves kept taut by their work, they have to bear patiently with complaints and protests which may or may not be justified, but are all too often couched in terms that are anything but considerate. Trunk operators are particularly exposed to mis-understanding and abuse owing to the urgency of many of the calls they handle. Yet it was precisely the Spanish trunk-exchange operators who, a few years ago, found an ideal answer to their professional trials.

'The last long distance calls are usually cleared by about four in the morning. From then on, duty operators have little to do but stand by until another day begins. One night, as the silent hours dragged slowly on, it occurred to an operator in Saragossa to suggest saying a rosary with her colleagues. From then on, at five every morning, operators all over the Peninsula connected with Saragossa—city of Our Lady of the Pillar, Patron Saint of Spain—covered the sleeping country with a network of prayer.

'As a commentator observed at the time, the trunk exchange operators could not have found a more Christian reply to the discourtesies they had had to accept during the day. Their initiative was also a small but attractive way of turning the instruments of material progress to spiritual account.'

Our Indian operator revealed that India is more 'Christian' than the Christians; when at one in the morning, we had hysterics on the telephone and revealed that it was a matter of a Lost Child, she replied crisply, 'You should have said so before. I should naturally have given you priority. Now the lines are closed but I will use the emergency line.' Ten minutes later we were talking to Victoria's sister. Victoria's aeroplane was grounded at Darwin; but even Darwin was better than limbo.

Customs and Excise

'Other ships, other long splices'; or to paraphrase a French commonplace, '*Autres lieux, autres moeurs*'. Landing at Auckland, New Zealand, in brilliant sunshine, we found ourselves among a people of shoe fetishists. The officers were not interested in tobacco, alcohol, perfume; but had we any shoes, apart from those on our feet which were examined suspiciously. We had; fourteen pairs between the two of us. And where had we come from? Brazil, Argentina and Mexico. That, as a Cockney friend of ours used to say, tore it. Our shoes, including those on our feet, were taken from us and there we stood in, respectively, socks and stockings, until our footwear, fumigated, was very civilly returned to us—in a polythene bag. Could we be told what all this was about? Certainly. New Zealanders are, like George the Third, concerned to avoid a murrain among the horned cattle. God knows what viruses, what bacteria, we had carried across the world on our shoes.

Customs at the Customs vary widely: in the Australian state of Victoria they don't give a damn about shoes but books worry them terribly. A copy of John Gould Cozzens anodyne *By Love Possessed* was sufficient to get me held up for quarter of an hour while the Victorian *Index Expurgatorio* was consulted; a copy of Violette Leduc's *La Bâtarde* passed muster, although given the archaic *moeurs* of Melbourne a book in French should have been suspect.

In Ceylon they are not interested in heroin, as in Boston, or the usual contraband, or shoes or books; but you have to 'declare' every scrap of jewellery, and all your money; then when you leave they can try to equate the value of the sapphires you've bought—they are very cheap there—with the amount of money you have left. The discrepancy is the sum of money you have exchanged on the black currency market. As any Ceylonese jeweller will accept an ordinary English cheque, this system of currency control fails to work—just like any other system of exchange restriction.

Entering the USSR there was no attempt at any kind of Customs check; it was as easy and quick as crossing a Common Market frontier. The Spanish Customs officers feel obliged to make a pretence of control, but they are so obviously bored with and contemptuous of their job they constitute no serious obstacle to the cool smuggling tourist. But Portugal is another matter entirely; that lovely country is a very ancient bureaucracy; it is necessary to find paper work for an enormously inflated staff of clerks; so everything, every declaration, every statement has to be written down. A similar spirit has spread to the Brazilians: the Customs examination at Rio de Janeiro is a kind of pandemonium. You step off the aircraft after an all night flight and are instantly involved—at a temperature and humidity both around the 100 mark—in sweating, shouting uproar. Half-uniformed women with Russian figures and black moustaches take away your passport, and ultimately restore it, without explanation. Suitcases are turned inside out by scowling officers. Nothing comes of it; it is all in play. The Brazilians have none of the calm, the dignity of the old country, qualities one learns to admire in Lisbon and Oporto, or in the superb novels of Eça de Queiros. But there's no harm in them.

I once made the appalling mistake of declaring some contraband on my way into Italy. I had, on top of the car, an enormous load of live plants—young trees, shrubs and perennials for a garden I was planting for some friends, in Italy. This was so prominent that it did not occur to me, when asked if I had anything to declare, to say NO. I said Yes. With urgently pleading eyes the officer, who as an intelligent man and moreover an Italian, knew that his job was ridiculous, asked if I were quite *sure*. As I had gone to enormous trouble to obtain phytosanitary certificates, special transit permission for France, and a letter permitting me to import plants, from the Italian authorities, I insisted on declaring my plants. Three days later

I was still waiting for the phytosanitary officer from Milan and had been driven, by the overwhelming volume of incomprehensible regulations, to employ the expensive services of an export-import agent. All I had to do was to give the only sensible answer to the world-wide Customs' question: Nothing.

Only at British and United States entry ports do Customs officers still, with pompous solemnity, take the job of restricting liberty seriously: the chief difference is that the British officers have pretty manners; the Americans act tough. In the United States a traveller has the right to demand that a Customs officer put on clean white gloves before searching his luggage; an acquaintance of mine, fussy about his silk shirts, and in a bad temper, tried it: five hours later they at last found the official white gloves.

From Kandy to Nuwara Eliya

This is some of the most beautiful country I have seen anywhere in the world, let alone Ceylon. The distance is only about forty-eight miles and in the course of it you climb over six thousand feet; and five miles on, at the pretty little botanic garden of Hakgala, one is at seven thousand feet. The country is all steep gorges, narrow valleys, rocky outcrops, superlative trees. For at least twenty-five miles it is planted, in suitable places, with tea; the plantations are steeply terraced and even very rocky land is used, the biggest, deeply rooted rocks being left *in situ*. Because the way tea is picked gives the whole plantation a flat top like an evenly clipped hedge, this rock-and-foliage landscape is very remarkable, as if an Italian gardener had turned planter. The terraces and odd corners of fertile land are often revetted with roughly dressed stone. There are streams and waterfalls everywhere, and small, uncultivated pieces of land are rich with wild flowers most of which I did not know. There are very beautiful ferns, including a tree-fern and a big maidenhair fern.

As one rises there are glorious views of distant mountains over immense distances. Tea pickers move among the bushes with baskets on their backs; most of them are Tamils, paid about three rupees a day. Their poverty is atrocious and their squalid hutments reminded me of the worst kind of hop-pickers' camps, in Kent, before the Second World War.

New English

Who on earth is responsible for translating menus into English for the tourists? It is inconceivable that large, often official organisations have nobody with a proper knowledge of English to turn to. I have already referred to the Soviet example 'sturgeon cooked in spit'—and yet the Russians are a nation of linguists. The Spaniards are not, but on the other hand tourism is much more important and more catered for in Spain than in Russia; yet we found 'Crab's Cream' on the menu of one grand hotel, and on that of another 'good girl soup'. I forget what it was like. One can only conclude that it is done on purpose, deliberately to play up to the well known fact that everybody in the world thinks that foreigners are funny.

Brick Earth

Good fruit-growing country, where the orchards look handsome and shops in the country towns sell prime fruit, whether apples, pears, or peaches, very often also produces good red brick architecture. I noticed this dual likeness in, for example, East Kent in England, the country round Verona in Northern Italy, and the country round Lerida in Spain. The reason is not difficult to find: all kinds of fruit trees flourish in brick earths and wherever bricks have been made for centuries there will be a pleasing traditional style of building with them. And as the farmers, where the climate is suitable, will also be exploiting the brick earth in the most profitable way, you get the same pattern repeated. In the region of Lerida, however, unlike Kent or the Veronese, the brick earth is patchy; where it occurs, irrigation produces rich green orchards but between these areas of fertile land is arid, eroded country, buff and grey and dusty, with cliff-faces showing curious stratification. The flora of this eroded country is very poor by comparison with another country, which, in other respects, it closely resembles—the Argentine *pampa seca*. The *pampa seca* has a rich flora of cacti; but that family is confined to America. Might it not be used to rehabilitate the arid parts of Spain? It would be difficult to find species hardy enough to survive the savage Spanish winters. As soon as you begin to climb out of the Leridan plain, the flora becomes richer, chiefly of aromatic sub-shrubs and small trees, including myrtle.

Roadside Trees

Only in France is the planting of roadside trees done with sufficient thoroughness and an admirable choice of species. Yet nothing so much improves the beauty of roads, or more effectively makes an ugly road sightly. And nothing contributes more to the comfort of travellers. The practice of planting highways seems to be an ancient one in all civilizations: of Kublai Khan, Marco Polo says:

'At both sides of the public roads he causes trees to be planted, of a kind that become large and tall, and being only two paces asunder, they serve (besides the advantage of their shade in summer) to point out the road (when the ground is covered with snow); which is of great assistance and affords much comfort to travellers. This is done along all the high roads where the nature of the soil admits of plantation; but when the way lies through sandy deserts or over rocky mountains, where it is impossible to have trees, he orders stones to be placed and columns to be erected as marks for guidance. He also appoints officers of rank, whose duty it is to see that all these are properly arranged and the roads constantly kept in good order. Besides the motives that have been assigned for these plantations, it may be added that the grand khan is the more disposed to make them from the circumstances of his diviners and astrologers having declared that those who plant trees are rewarded with long life.'

The Incas planted Molle trees beside some of their post roads and this practice of using fruit trees instead of shade and shelter trees like planes and poplars is not uncommon in eastern Europe; in Bulgaria there are roads lined with cherry trees over distances as great as fifty miles. In this respect Britain is very backward, which seems a shame in a country famous for the beauty of its trees.

Rice and Motorcars in Southern India

In southern India in the neighbourhood of Madras and in Ceylon, village women have no flat, clean floor on which to spread their rice to dry after threshing, so they use the road, metalled for the benefit of the motor-car, which provides an ideal surface for that purpose. All through a village the surface of the road is covered—we saw this in the month of January—with very neat parallelograms of rice grains, not more, probably, than one grain deep; so that every grain is exposed to air and sunshine. This, of course, causes considerable inconvenience to drivers but I never saw one so inconsiderate as to drive over the rice; drivers of buses, private cars and trucks very carefully avoid the squares and oblongs of rice, most of the women having the sense to leave clear just enough of the road surface for a thoroughfare. We were much struck with the considerate gentleness of drivers in this avoidance of the villagers' rice. They are the same people who, with apparent indifference, leave scores of people to die of starvation every night in every great city of India.

Indian Temple Art

Nothing we saw in India—and one can see little of that country's treasure and beauties in an ordinary working visit—delighted us more than Kancheepuram and Mahabalipuram. In remote antiquity seven cities of India were famous for their holiness so that a pilgrimage to any of them conferred merit on the pilgrim: they are Ayodya, Mathura, Maya, Kasi, Avanti, Dwaraka and, above all, Kancheepuram celebrated for the worship of both

Siva and Vishnu. Among the city's sons are many philosophers, exponents of Visishtadvaita, of Saiva Siddhanta and other religious systems; and numerous artists also, including one of the three famous composers of Carnatic music. The heart of the city's philosophical, religious and artistic life is the temple called Sri Ekambaranathar (Eka Amrar Nathar = Lord of the Supreme Mango Tree). This temple is so ancient that its oldest parts are prehistoric: here is the legend of its foundation.

Siva asked the goddess Parvati to make a symbol of himself in the sand of the stream called Kampa flowing by Kachee Mayanam. She did so and worshipped the symbol with love, piety and devotion. The Lord Siva, to draw the attention of others to Parvati's loving devoutness, caused freshets in the stream; but these threatened to wash her symbol away and she, to save it, hugged it to her breast. Siva was so delighted that he appeared to her in person, married her, and granted her many blessings: thus the place became for ever blessed with his presence.

The temple is immensely rich in the most vividly lively and beautiful carvings of many epochs. The whole surface of its stones seethes and throbs with marvellous life in every aspect. We have never seen sculpture which so seizes and holds one's fascinated attention.

There is, growing in the second *brakara* of the temple, behind the Moolasthanam, the sacred eponymous mango tree, a remarkable specimen of *Mangifera indica*. Its dimensions are only estimated, for its sacredness forbids exact measurement, but the trunk is said to be twenty-five feet in girth, its height sixty feet, and its age 2500 years. Fruitful on all four of its principal branches, the fruit of each branch is supposed to have a different taste.

Mahabalipuram is an ancient Pallava seaport, enormously rich in beautiful sculpture, much of it over two thousand years old and all of it vigorously animated with that dancing, pulsing, turbulent life which makes such an impression on the beholder at Kancheepuram. One of the most astounding of these works is the great bas-relief called Arjuna's penance; it is carved on the face of a boulder 90 feet long and 20 feet high; it is a writhing pageant of divine beings, *gandharvas*, men, serpents, elephants, lions, leopards, monkeys, cats, mice, birds, and a figure of Siva with a beggar performing a penance called *tapas*. It is impossible to convey the extraordinary movement imparted to the stone by the skill of the artists, especially in the great frieze of elephants with their calves, and in such detail as a deer scratching its face with a hind hoof.

But this is only one link; there are, scattered over a quite small area, a score of rock carving groups, pavilions, temples, all alive with the joy and terror of life caught and for ever set down in stone: Krishna holds aloft a whole hill with its people and animals to save them from floods sent by Indra; a family of monkeys pick salt from each other's skins; a cowherd milks his cow while she, her head sweetly turned and lowered, licks her calf; armed female guards, majestic and eternal, guard the cave Dranpadi. In one panel Vishnu, depicted with the mask of a wild boar, holds Laakshmi in his lap; and in another Vishnu measures the universe with his limbs. In the cave called Mahishasuramardini there is a tremendous battle, the principals being a goddess superbly mounted on a fiercely embattled lion, and the buffalo-demon Mahishasura.

But the riches, in life and art, of this shrine are not to be compassed in writing short of many volumes. We have yet to see them surpassed.

The Small Hours Halt

There is a curious sad pleasure in the late night or early morning breaks in long flights; briefly you are afoot again, in a familiar place made cold and strange by lights wan against an early dawn; or in a place you have never been to and probably never will go to again and which this half-hour midnight touch-down hardly entitles you to add to your score of places visited. Leaving London late at night to fly by way of Paris to Rio de Janeiro, you touch down at Madrid; it is two in the morning but the tourist shop is open for business and a man with the yellow Spanish face of a grief-stricken mule is offering mantillas. Nobody buys; you are given a free coffee and add to it an expensive whisky. Five minutes later you are uncomfortably half asleep again between earth and stars: and that, for thousands of travellers will be for ever the sum of Madrid, one of Europe's loveliest cities. Papeete, at one a.m., on the way from Mexico to Auckland, New Zealand. The police officer's uniform is startlingly French; you lay in a supply of duty-free Gauloises and drink a cognac; for five minutes you pace the richly-planted terraces, marvelling at the strange colours of tropical flowers and foliage seen by electric light and recall all the doubtless misleadingly glamorous things you have read about these islands. You have been to Papeete; and never seen it. There was, too, the time when we made a dawn landing, on the way from South Africa to Europe, in Addis Ababa, and when the apple-green and flame-gold glory of the sky over a vast pale plain made us long to miss the aeroplane and remain for a while in Ethiopia: all we ever saw that was proper to that ancient land was its gorgeous dawn sky and the strange shapes of primitive musical instruments which a passenger, joining our aircraft there, had been collecting.

It is curious how, during such brief, nocturnal halts, you speak to each other in lowered voices, smile but do not laugh, put down cup or glass with deliberation—as if not to disturb the sleep of the people into whose land you have swooped: an absurdity, of course; God knows, if your screaming jets don't wake them, your voice will never do it. But there it is, a kind of courtesy, a kind of apology for intrusion.

Switzerland in the Andes

In South America, whenever you are in mountain-and-lake country you are apt to be back in Switzerland or Austria. Perhaps migrants leave home only to find it, with improvements. Our room in San Carlos de Bariloche, Argentina (near to the Chilean frontier), looked out onto Lake Nahuel Huapi and its surrounding frieze of mountains. One saw at a glance why immigrants from the Alpine countries would feel at home in these Andean foothills. It was early November but spring had not reached that altitude yet and it was very cold. Going into the town to shop, we were in Switzerland—the smell of sawn planks and wooden houses; the chalet-style buildings, the very wide eaves to deal with winter's heavy snows; the well-made but bundly clothes of thick knitwear and leather; the pastry shops, smelling of hot chocolate; the winter sports shops; the German names. Argentina, Chile, all Patagonia, have scores of such places. In a curious way, it's disappointing: one does not go to the Andes to see Interlaken. Needless to add that further north, the *cordillera* is the very Andes; but here it is the Alps.

But at least the flora is very different: Bariloche is famous for its flowers and they do not disappoint. We were too early for *mutisia*, the great red and orange climbing daisies; and the notros (*Embothrium ssp.*) were not, of course in flower. A two hour trip on a steamer across lake Nahuel Huapi took us into rain forest country where *Lapageria* was flowering and the most gorgeous *Berberis darwinii* as well as other barberries. There is a beautiful *Fuchsia*, apparently an endemic, and a very remarkable parasitic plant, growing like mistletoe but the bushes much larger and with vivid crimson scarlet flowers which look, at first glance, proteacious though the plant—*Phrygilantus tentrandrus*—belongs to the *Lorantaceae*. The vernacular name is *Quintral del Alamo*. Other plants natural to this region are the lovely pale crimson rose called *La Mosqueta* (*Rosa rubiquerea*); the big Chilean strawberry from which our own large-fruited strawberries derive; *Oenothera propinqua*, the evening primrose which Argentines call *Don Diego de la noche*; the spectacular *Desfontainea* like a holly bush covered with orange flowers; *Topa-Topa*, a charming little calceolaria; the deep crimson *Ourisia* and the equally charming *Mitrarias* and *Asterantheras*. All this quickly neutralises the Swiss quality of San Carlos.

The lake littoral and one of its islands have a small tree, peculiar and confined to this province. I took it for a myrtle, but this *Arrayan* is not a true myrtle, but *Myrcengenia apiculata*. The island of these dwarfish, immensely ancient, oddly 'quaint' looking trees was used by the late Walt Disney as the setting for 'Bambi'.

Canary Discovery

We are accustomed to believe that the age of discovery and colonisation by Europeans of the world beyond Europe began late in the 15th century. There were earlier European seafarers, not to mention such overland travellers as Marco Polo; and it has often seemed to me strange that we have taken so little interest in the discovery of the Canary Islands. For although there was some rather vague knowledge of them in antiquity, they had to be rediscovered by Christian Europe. The geographer Strabo says this:

'The poets make mention of the islands of the Blest, and we know that even now they may be seen not far from the extremity of Mauritania, opposite Cadiz. Now I say that those who pointed out these things were the Phoenicians who before the time of Homer had possession of the best parts of Africa and Spain.'

But although, according to Plutarch, in his *Life of Sertorius*, the Romans knew of these same islands a thousand years later, and King Juba the Second of Mauritania sent an expedition to rediscover them, and Pliny calls them the Fortunate Islands, they had been quite lost sight and memory of: the Moors knew of them as the Islands of Khaledat. But the point is that while Moorish pirates, and pirates or slavers from Majorca, almost certainly raided the islands for Guanche slaves—the Guanches, last remnant of the Cro-Magnon race whose brilliant artistic talent is still manifest at Lascaux and Magdalenia, being white, fetched high prices in the Aragonese and Moorish slave-markets—still the islands had no official existence in the eyes of geographers: like other realities they were known to people but not to science.

However, there was one officially testified rediscovery of the archipelago before the 15th century. The evidence is in the *Portulano Mediceo*, bearing the date 1351, in the *Bibliotheca Laurentiana* at Florence. It is, apparently, Genoese work; and on one of its maps the easterly group of the archipelago is shown, with the arms of Genoa against the island of Lanzanote. Now this name was simply the Christian name of the island's rediscoverer, Lansaroto, or Lanceloto (that is, Lancelot) Malocello, a Genoese merchant seaman. The tower which he and his men built on the island was found still standing, its only post-Neolithic artefact—by the Norman Jean de Bethencourt, first conqueror of the islands, when he landed there in 1402.

Canary Discovery

What we do not know exactly is the date of Lancelot Malocello's rediscovery: but we can get near to it. A passage in Petrarch says that an armed Genoese fleet found and visited the Fortunate Islands, *a patrum memoria*. Petrarch was born in 1304. His *a patrum memoria* can hardly refer to a period less than a generation ago, which fixes Malocello's voyage at about 1280; and if Petrarch's phrase means what it would commonly be used to mean, the date must be even earlier, say about or before the middle of the 13th century.

Well before the end of the 14th century Portuguese kings had sent expeditions to the islands, almost certainly commanded by Genoese sea captains. As early as 1317 King Denis the Labourer appointed the Genoese Emmanuele Pezagno admiral of his fleet with succession to his sons. In a letter to Pope Clement VI, in 1334, in answer to a brief requesting the King of Portugal to support Don Luis de la Cerda to whom His Holiness had granted royal authority over the Fortunate Islands with the title of Prince of Fortune, the King replied that he had already sent an expedition there. It was doubtless commanded by Pezagno or one of his sons. Here, moreover, is an account by Boccaccio of an expedition to the islands in 1341.[1]

'On the first of July . . . two vessels furnished by the King of Portugal with all the necessary provisions and accompanied by a smaller vessel well armed and manned by Florentines, Genoese, Castillians and other Spaniards, among whom were naturally included Portugese, for the word Hispani included all inhabitants of the Peninsula, set sail from Lisbon and put out into the open sea. They took with them horses, arms and warlike engines for storming towns and castles in search of those islands commonly called the "Rediscovered" . . .'

They must have been disappointed; seige engines were not much use against Neolithic savages. They brought back some

[1] The MS was discovered by Sebastiano Ciampi in 1827. Boccacio had the facts from letters written by two Florentine merchants settled in Sevilla.

natives and a cargo of goat skins, seal skins and other island produce. They landed on Fuerteventura, were afraid to land on Grand Canary because the people, though apparently friendly, were very numerous, but later on the south side, landed among vegetable gardens and fig plantations, and stole an idol from a small stone temple. They sailed round to Hierro, landed on La Gomera and killed some large pigeons. They sighted La Palma and were deterred from landing on Tenerife by a phenomenon which alarmed them: up among the snows of the great peak which they over-estimated at 30 thousand feet—it is actually 12 thousand—they saw a black rock.

'. . . On top of which was a mast as large as a ship's mast, with a yard and a lateen sail set upon it. The sail when blown out by the wind took the form of a shield, and soon afterwards it would seem to be lowered, together with the mast, as if on board a vessel, then again it was raised, and again would sink, and so alternately . . .'

But the effective rediscovery of the islands was the Norman knight's, the adventurer Jean de Bethencourt, a true traveller if ever there was one, for he had lands and castles and a beautiful young wife at home and had no need to seek his fortune. Bethencourt's work was effective because he conquered Fuerteventura and Lanzarote and settled there with Norman peasants and tradesmen (1402–5). If the islands are today Spanish, not French, it is because Jean's worthless nephew and heir, Maciot, sold them to a Spanish nobleman, as well as to several other people including Henry the Navigator; and because the much more fertile and western group was conquered, after several defeats and nearly a century, by Spaniards. Bethencourt's story can be read in the book which two of his companions, his chaplains, Jean le Verrier and Pierre Bontier, wrote. It is one of the most curious travel books I have ever read.[1]

[1] *The Canarian.* Hakluyt Society 1872. A splendid 3 vol. critical edition in the original French and in Spanish was published by the University of La Laguna, Tenerife, in 1956.

Over the Andes

The most spectacular aeroplane journey we have yet done was from San Carlos de Bariloche in Argentina over the *Cordillera de los Andes*, to Puerto Montt in Chile. The mountains here are not the giants they are further north: one flies between Tronador, 11,352 feet to the north and Hornopiren 5,479 feet to the south. But on a bitterly cold day of vividly blue sky and brilliant sunshine, dry and sparkling as a diamond, the view from the Chilean Airways *Caravelle* was almost limitless. It cannot have been less than two hundred miles in both directions, that is north and south. To the north were the peaks of Lanin (12,270), Villarca (9,317), Jaima (10,040) and lesser mountains; the peaks to the south, Corcovado and Comica and others, are not so high, mostly about 7,000 to 7,500 feet.

The flight began in farce: a young American woman, noisily garrulous, twitching and jerking in a kind of unwholesome nervous excitement, insisting on talking vile Spanish to officials who spoke excellent English, and loudly declaring her mission to write a series of articles for some middle-western newspaper, was unable to pay her airport tax because the official would not change her ten dollar travellers' cheques. The *bureau de change* was not open. I offered the lady the necessary dollar and was taken aback to be informed that she did not accept money from strange men. She tried the bar, first announcing that she was not accustomed to enter bars. She had a remarkable and totally mistaken belief that her habits and feelings were of general interest. Perhaps in her own town, despite her whey face of the chronically constipated, and her tow hair, she was a beauty and a young woman of consequence; In San Carlos she was not. Something, possibly her Spanish, so offended the barman that he too refused her cheque and she was obliged to come back to me, after causing a scene and by then nearly hysterical, and accept my dollar; this time she offended every

bilingual Argentino and Chilean within the range of her penetrating voice, by announcing that she could safely take money
from me as I was an Englishman.

The flight was marvellous beyond words; the vast picture
framed in the *Caravelle* windows was all in white and blue—
true heavenly blue not only of the cloudless sky, but of the lakes
set like enchanting toy lakes amongst the peaks—Lake Rinco,
Lake Rununco and Lake Llanquihue before us, Nahuel Huapi
behind us. And these true blue jewels were set exquisitely in the
folds and jags of the snowy *cordillera*. We lunched, as we stared
out and down, on salty sea-urchins and a superb Chilean red
wine; the steak, second course, was entirely uneatable even
by those with good, young Argentine (i.e. exclusively carnivor-
ous) teeth. But given the scenery, the wine and the startling
beauty of the stewardesses, the steak's toughness was un-
important.

An advantage of scenery seen from an aeroplane is that it is
not there for long; now you see it, now you don't. You see a
sublimely serene, a transcendentally tranquil lake, hung in space
in the hole on the top of a colossal buttress supporting a ten
thousand foot mountain; you see it for just long enough to realise
that no man can ever possibly have set foot on its shores. Then it is
ten, twenty miles behind you; your intrusion has been as brief as
it was remote. Spectacular scenery is one of my delights; to drive
a car through high alpine country a pleasure unpalling. But I
cannot stand long and stare at it; certainly not for long enough to
realise that it is meaningless, a pattern made by accident.
Nature is only enduringly interesting in detail and given the
kind of knowledge which gives the beholder easy access to a
chain of associations. The sublime—and I have looked upon
Kanchenjunga at dawn—very quickly becomes a bore.

By the way, the excitable American maiden repaid my dollar
at Puerto Montt.

Wineless Mexico

Mexico City is one of the most pleasing capitals we have seen. But if only they would resist American influence to the extent of serving wine in restaurants in the European or South American way, as a matter of course. It's not impossible to get wine but you have to make a slight fuss; and the wine is unjustifiably dear. This is all the stranger in that Mexico was the first viticultural country in the New World:

'One of the problems which faced the Conquistadors in their conquests and colonizations in America was that of providing a supply of wine for the Mass. It should not be thought of as a minor problem; to the Spaniard of the sixteenth century it was of the very first importance; it is literally true to say that the Catholic European could not live his life with anything like peace of mind in the total absence of *Vitis vinifera*. It was quite as important to the sixteenth-century Spaniards as it ever was to the sectaries of Dionysus or Flufluns. Hernan Cortes in particular was a man of fanatical piety who had to be restrained by his own chaplains from destruction of idols at dangerously inexpedient moments, and from mass-conversion of Aztec and other natives of Anahuac, which his religious advisers knew to be worthless.

'The ships from Spain carried a provision of wine, of course. It does not seem (see below) that there were plantings of the vine in Hispaniola or Cuba, the first parts of America to be colonized. Most of the ships coming from Spain brought wine from the Canary Islands, where all outward-bound ships and most inward-bound stopped to water. The ships were small and few, some were lost at sea, cargo space must have been extremely valuable and wine is a bulky cargo, although one way to bring it was as ballast. It was, in short, obvious that the sooner vines were planted in the New World the better.

'Although the conquest, even of the relatively small area of

Mexico in the immediate neighbourhood of the city, was not really complete until 1530, Cortes first sent to Spain for vine-cuttings in 1522, at the same time as he sent for other useful plants. It is from the following brief reference to this transaction that we can, I think, conclude that there were then no vines to be had in Hispaniola or Cuba: '*De las islas del America Trans-porta [Cortes] el ganado mayor y menor, las canes dulces, que el immortal Colon habia llevado a las Canarias, con otras plantas que nacen en aquellos climas calientes. De Espana [llevo] las vides, morales, peros y manzanos.*'

'It is obvious that had Cortes been able to get his vines from the islands, with that sugar-cane which 'the immortal Columbus had brought from the Canaries', he would have done so. As it was, he had to fetch his cuttings, with apples, pears and mulberries from Spain. His agent there was his father Martin Cortes. But the Conquistador did not stop at that; as soon as he began the building of the new Mexico City, near the site of the great Venice-style water-city of Tenochtitlan which he had more or less destroyed, he advised the new Governor, who had been sent out from Spain because the Council of the Indies did not trust him, to require all ships entering the port of Vera Cruz from Spain to bring with them a quota of plants and seeds. But the only plant which he specifically ruled must be planted, while he himself still had control of New Spain, was the vine. For he had made *repartimientos*, that is, grants of land and Indians as slaves to work it, conditional on the planting of a quota of vines. This regulation was one of the by-laws of the new Mexico City municipality, drawn up while that city was still building, in 1524. For every hundred Indians of the *repartimiento*, a thousand vines had to be planted, and they must, moreover, be the best obtainable.'[1]

[1] Hyams, E., *Dionysus*. Thames & Hudson, London and Macmillan, New York, 1965 drawing upon Cavo, Andres *Historia de Mexico*, in the edition of Father F. J. Burrus, S.J., Mexico City, 1959.

Travelling for Wine

Travellers with a taste for vineyard country think of Burgundy, as they pass from one vine estate, one great wine name, to the next, as clearly one of France's richest provinces. It was not always so. True, the *pagus Arebrignus*, the latter-day Côtes de Beaune and Côtes de Nuits country, had already long been famous for its wines in the third century: it does not follow that they enriched it, and here is a translation of part of a public speech once made on this subject:

'This famous canton, well known for its wine growing, is very far from deserving the envy with which it is regarded. On the one hand it has its back to a land of mountains and impenetrable forests, where wild beasts have their hidden lairs. On the other hand it overhangs a great flat plain extending to the Saône. True, it is claimed that this plain was formerly flourishing, but that was at a time when the labour of cultivating it was never relaxed, and when every farmer kept his drains free of obstruction, thus clearing the land of water. But nowadays, as a consequence of the devastations, the ditches are obstructed and these same lowlands which formerly owed their fertility to their situation are falling back into a stage of bog and marsh.

'As for the vineyards, those vineyards which are so much admired by people ignorant of their real condition, they are so exhausted by age that they hardly respond at all to the care we lavish on them. The vine-stocks whose age we no longer know, have by the interlacing of their thousands of roots formed a solid platform which prevents deep digging between them, so that for want of sufficient soil-covering the layers[1] are exposed to the rain which drowns them and the sun which burns them. And here we have not the advantage common in Aquitaine and other provinces of being able to find almost anywhere room to

---

[1] 'Layering' was used to reroot and so renew the vines.

plant new vineyards, crowded as we are between low-lying land
where frosts are to be feared . . .'
The speech was made by the Rhetor of Autun in 312 AD before
the Emperor Constantine.[1] Maybe we should take it, though,
with a pinch of salt, for its object was to obtain a remission of
taxes, in which it succeeded.

Africa Circumnavigated

We are too apt to think of our fifteenth and seventeenth centuries
as the age of discovery by sea voyaging. But there were others.
Some palaeontologists believe that in prehistoric times the
advanced Neolithic or Chalcolithic societies of south-east
Asia traded across the Pacific with more backward peoples in
what is now Peru. And coastal shipping, or perhaps one should
say boating was important in Neolithic Europe. There are, of
course, no documents to show the true extent and nature of
such seafaring. But in the fifth century B.C. Herodotus was
able to write thus:
'. . . As for Libya, we know it to be washed on all sides by the
sea, except where it is attached to Asia. This discovery was first
made by Necos, the Egyptian king, who on desisting from the
canal which he had begun building between the Nile and the
Arabian Gulf, sent to sea a number of ships manned by
Phoenicians, with orders to make for the Pillars of Hercules,
and return to Egypt through them, and by the Mediterranean.
The Phoenicians took their departure from Egypt by way of the
Erythraean Sea, and so sailed into the southern ocean. When
autumn came, they went ashore, wherever they might happen

[1] It is given in full in *Panégyriques latins*. Vol 2. Ed. Galletier, E.

to be, and having sown a tract of land with corn, waited until the grain was fit to cut. Having reaped it, they again set sail; and thus it came to pass that two whole years went by, and it was not till the third year that they doubled the Pillars of Hercules, and made good their voyage home. On their return, they declared— I for my part do not believe them, but perhaps others may— that in sailing round Libya they had the sun upon their right hand. In this way was the extent of Libya first discovered.'

For Libya, read, of course, Africa. And that these Phoenicians really had done what they said they had done is clear from that business of the sun being on their right hand—a thing that always bothers me in the southern hemisphere.

This was not the only sea voyage of its kind in the fifth century B.C. In about 425 B.C. Hanno, one of the Suffetes of Carthage—a Suffete was a kind of Consul, an elected Chief Magistrate—commanded a voyage of discovery down the west coast of Africa. Here is his account of it:

'The Carthaginians decided that Hanno should sail beyond the Pillars of Heracles and found cities of Libyophoenicians. He set sail with sixty penteconters and about 3,000 men and women and provisions and other necessaries. After sailing beyond the Pillars for two days we founded the first city which we called Thymiaterion. Below it was a large plain. Sailing thence westward we came to Soloeis, a Libyan promontory covered with trees. There we founded a temple to Poseidon. Journeying eastward for half a day we reached a lake not far from the sea, covered with a great growth of tall reeds, where elephants and many other wild animals fed. A day's sea journey beyond this lake we founded cities on the coast called Karikon Teichos, Gytte, Akra, Melitta and Arambys. Passing on from there we came to the large river Lixos, flowing from Libya, beside which nomads called Lixitae pastured their flocks. We stayed some time with them and became friends. Inland from there dwelt inhospitable Ethiopians in a land ridden with wild beasts and hemmed in by great mountains. They say that the Lixos flows down from there and that among these mountains Troglodytes of strange appearance dwell, who according to the Lixitae can run more swiftly than horses. Taking interpreters from the Lixitae we sailed south along the desert shore for two days and then for one day eastward and found a small island 5 stades (c. 1 km.) in circumference at the farther end of a gulf. We made a settlement there and called it Cerne. We judged from our journey that it was directly opposite Carthage, for the voyage from Carthage to the Pillars and from there to Cerne seemed alike. From here sailing up a big river called Chretes we reached a lake, in which were three islands bigger than Cerne. Completing a day's sail from here we came to the end of the lake, overhung by some very high mountains crowded with savages clad in skins of wild beasts, who stoned us and beat us off and prevented us from disembarking. Sailing from there we came to another wide river, teeming with crocodiles and hippopotamuses. We turned again from there and came back to Cerne. We sailed south for twelve days from there, clinging to the coast, which was all along occupied by Ethiopians who did not stay their ground but fled from us. Their speech was unintelligible, even to our Lixitae. On the last day we came to anchor by some high mountains clad with trees whose wood was sweet-smelling and mottled. Sailing round these for two days we reached an immense gulf, on either shore of which was a plain where by night we saw big and little fires flaming up at intervals everywhere. Taking on water here, we sailed on for five days along the coast until we came to a great bay which our interpreters called the Horn of the West. In it was a large island in a salt-water lake, within which was another island where we disembarked. By day we could see nothing but a forest, but by night we saw many fires burning and we heard the sound of flutes and beating of cymbals and drums and a great din of voices. Fear came upon us and the soothsayers bade us leave the island. We sailed thence in haste and skirted a fiery coast replete with burning incense. Great streams of fire and lava poured down into the sea and the land was unapproachable because of the heat. We left there hurriedly in fear and sailing for four days we saw the land by night full of flames. In the middle was a high flame taller than the rest, reaching, as it seemed, the stars. By day it was seen to be a very high mountain called the Chariot of the Gods. Thence sailing for three days past fiery lava we reached a gulf called the Horn of the South. At the further end of this bay was an island, like the first, with a lake, within which was another island full of savages. By far the greater number were women with shaggy bodies, whom our interpreters called Gorillas. Chasing them we were unable to catch any of the men, all of whom, being used to climbing precipices, got away, defending themselves by throwing stones. But we caught three women, who bit and mangled those who carried them off, being unwilling to follow them. We killed them, however, and flayed them and brought their skins back to Carthage. For we did not sail further as our supplies gave out.'

The Discovery of the Galapagos

In the middle of the fifteenth century Topa Inca Yupanqui, heir to the vast Inca Empire ruled by his illustrious father the Sapa Inca Pachacuti, was engaged in rounding off the Empire by conquering the Quitu nation whose capital Quito is now the capital of Ecuador. In Quito the Inca prince heard of certain islands which, according to the Spanish chronicler Sarmiento, were called Hahua-chumbi and Nina-chumbi. They were said to be rich in gold and in people with whom the Quitu carried on trade by means of balsa rafts. Topa Inca made up his mind to visit these islands; Sarmiento gives, as his motive, the prince's wish 'to challenge his star and see whether it would favour him on sea as on land.' Topa had a fleet of balsa rafts made and rigged and with a detachment of his army acting as marines, set sail for what Sarmiento, their Spanish discoverer, believed to be the Galapagos Islands. Palaeontologists and historians long pooh-poohed the idea that the Galapagos had ever been populated by any people with a high culture. But when Thor Heyerdahl visited the islands he found Chimu-type potsherds.

Chimu was one of the great pre-Inca civilized and urban states of ancient Peru. Its capital city, Chan-Chan, built on the grid system, covered eleven square miles. I suppose it is possible that Chimu once had a colony on the Galapagos. But Cabello, another Spanish historian, says that Topa Inca returned from the islands after nine months with dark-skinned prisoners, much gold, and a brass throne. What are we to make of this? Probably nothing. But there's always that possibility of trans-Pacific trade with South-east Asia.

The Periplus of the Erythraean Sea

There are travel books of antiquity which, if we are not professional scholars, we never hear of and which are more fascinating in their evocation of travelling conditions in remote antiquity than those we are familiar with.

In about the year A.D. 80 a master mariner of Alexandria wrote a small handbook about sea-borne trade, which was perhaps intended as a guide book for men of his calling; it is known as *The Periplus of the Erythraean Sea* and is, of course, written in Greek. It is at least possible that the author's intention was to make more widely known a fairly recent discovery by the Greeks, a discovery which was to affect all travel and sea-borne trade enormously until the invention of marine steam engines about eighteen centuries later: the monsoon winds.

The discovery was not really Greek; a professional navigator of Alexandria, Hippalus by name, probably got the facts about the monsoon winds and how to make use of them from Arab seamen who had long been familiar with the phenomenon and been careful to keep their knowledge, and so a near-monopoly of sea-borne trade with India, to themselves. The Arabs perhaps originally had their knowledge of the monsoon winds and their uses from Indian seamen. At all events Hippalus, whose discovery the author of the *Periplus* publicised, put into Greek hands the means to compete at sea with Indian and Arabian merchantmen; and, incidentally, thereby to ruin the economies of several south Arabian kingdoms.

By following the advice of the *Periplus* Greek captains were able to cut the sailing time from Alexandria to Aden to three weeks. The passage to the nearst Indian ports, using the monsoon, was cut to two months.

Hippalus's 'discovery' was made about A.D. 45. For how long before that date had Dravidian and Arabian seamen been using their own much more ancient discovery of the same meteorological facts? Quite probably for eight centuries; at all events the beginning of the Red Sea-Indian Ocean trade has been placed by good authorities in the 7th century B.C.

The author of the *Periplus*, who offers such advice as that Muza (Mocha) '. . . imports both wheat and wine but not much because the country produces a fair amount of wheat and a larger amount of wine . . .' had himself carried cargoes to the Arab (Omani) colonies in what is now Tanzania; and, possibly, even as far as the mouth of the Ganges.

Amateur Plant Collecting

A gardener's holiday travels can be made much more exciting
by a little plant collecting in the wild. What used to be difficult
has been made easy by polythene; sealed into a polythene bag
plants or cuttings will live for weeks, since the closed bag
eliminates all loss of moisture and the plant remains turgid
for weeks.

I should hate to encourage indiscriminate plant collecting;
we have done enough damage to the environment already and
in the past fine species, for example the Royal Fern, have been
nearly exterminated by amateur collectors whose plants
usually died; the waste of plant life was wicked, and still is.
The rules should be: collect only plants you are certain you can
keep alive in your garden; never on any account collect a rare
plant, at most take some seed if there is any, or a small cutting;
in any case, always prefer a cutting or seeds to a rooted plant
where possible; put one or at the most two plants or cuttings
into each polythene bag, and do so with the minimum of delay;
keep sealed bags of cuttings or plants in a cool shaded place,
and never expose them to the sun even for a moment; have with
you a stout cardboard box for your bags of cuttings or plants,
so that they can be packed loose, not squashed. As soon as you
get home plant cuttings of young plants in the propagating case
immediately, and then keep the case closed for as long as you
dare and until the danger of wilting seems past.

Apart from a supply of polythene bags, the amateur plant
collector needs only two tools: a very sharp pocket-knife, and a
very strong, very narrow, pointed trowel or weeding tool of the
finest quality. Alpine shrubs and bulbs usually grow in hard-
packed, stony soils and it is very difficult to dig up a deeply-
growing bulb undamaged without the suitable tool.

Shrubs: it is rare to find, in the wild, a shrub superior to
garden varieties of the species; but it can happen: I have,

notably, found barberries—in the woods round Lake Nahuel Huapi in the Andes; the botanical species of alpine rhododendrons are often exquisite; and some wild roses are worth collecting. There are others. I do not, as a rule, dig up even small seedling shrubs, but take cuttings of half-ripened wood if the season is right. Seeds are a second possibility; in a very few cases (e.g. *Daphne*, *Prunus*, *Malus*) you *may* be able to cut scions suitable for grafting, but success is very doubtful.

Bulbs can be safely collected at any time of the year, even in full flower. Do not half dig the bulb, and then start tugging at the stem; get right down to the roots and work the bulb loose patiently; the same instructions, of course, for corms and rhyzomes. Never trim off the undamaged roots of a bulb, corm or rhizome; the thing will take twice or three times as long to begin growing again if you do. Bulbs entering their dormant season with their leaves dying down can be dried and packed in paper; bulbs in flower are often better collected into polythene bags and sealed, like cuttings, unless you are going to be away for a long time.

Perennials: at first thought there is not much point in collecting herbaceous perennials, since as a rule garden varieties are better. But there are exceptions, for instance the lucky holiday cruiser to Nepal may find a meconopsis he wants, or a primula with no seed pods; even in England I have found *Geraniums* I wanted a piece of. Look for a small seedling; it is much more likely to survive. Alternatively, where the clump is large, it is often possible to dig round and then cleanly cut off a rooted side piece. At the right time of year the skilful gardener can sometimes find viable cutting material.

But do remember those rules.

Mexico Games

One of the oddest sights we saw on our travels was that of people of both sexes being drilled in the great park surrounding the magnificent Museum of Anthropology in Mexico City. We were not at our best: we had been several days in the city before discovering why we were so sleepy, a little dizzy and slightly inclined to feel sick; we had forgotten that Mexico City is at an altitude of about eight thousand feet. The spectacle of a lot of rather sloppy looking young women, who moreover were sulky and of every shape which the human form can assume, being drilled by a magnificent female drill sergeant, a sort of Scandinavian goddess in ballet tights, was a distressing one. The men, separated, were shaping up rather better, which was natural enough since Mexican males, like those of every country in the world, save Britain, are used to suffering the indignity of being prepared, by military drill, for whatever slaughter in war their masters decide on. The spectacle continued to puzzle us— we were waiting for the Museum to open and had time to kill— until it was borne in on us that the motions of the young women, into which they were being driven by the Scandinavian goddess in tights, were a gross and clumsy caricature of some we had seen before—those of the drum-majorettes who, by their antics, help the citizens of the United States to elect a President and perhaps, for all I know, actually decide the issue of American elections.

But Mexican elections are more likely to be decided by a mixture of bribery and violence than by drum-majorettes and only later did we realise that these girls were being drilled for the Olympic Games parades.

Lost Days

Unless you are totally indifferent to time, or fully and consciously aware that the imposition of the week and of named days of the week on nature is a mere convenient convention, your first crossing of the International Date Line is curiously disconcerting. We flew over it on the way from Acapulco in Mexico to Auckland, New Zealand. We flew from Tuesday into Thursday, losing a Wednesday which is in some ways my favourite day. We felt cheated. And since we have never been back that way, and had a week with two Wednesdays, I have since been irrationally convinced that I have been robbed of a whole day of life. Naturally I *know* that I haven't, that there is no such thing, in nature, as Wednesday or a week. But I feel that I have and sympathise with those other foolish and ignorant people who, when England's government changed her from the Julian to the Gregorian calendar, believed they had been robbed of more than a week of life and adopted, almost as an election cry, the slogan, 'Give us back our eleven days.'

Pirates

Shipwreck has been almost eliminated from the hazards of travel although there are occasional disasters; train accidents, too, are few and casualties, when they do occur, are rarely numerous. Probably driving a car is by far the most dangerous form of modern travel. The principal air travel hazard seems to be hijacking, a form of piracy. But its dangers are hardly to be compared with those of the seventeenth and eighteenth century piracy. The navigator William Dampier gives the following lurid account of the French buccaneer known as l'Ollonais, 'distinguished even among that ruthless fraternity for ... pre-eminence in crime.'

'Little is known of his family but it appears that when a youth he was either kidnapped or left home under a form of engagement, then not uncommon in several countries in Europe, by which the adventurer agreed to serve a certain number of years in the colonies. This practice, which was termed *indenting*, continued until a very recent period and was liable to great abuses. Escaping from servitude, l'Ollonais joined the buccaneers. His address and courage soon rendered him so conspicuous that in a few years he was the owner of two canoes and commanded twenty-two men. With this small force he captured a Spanish frigate on the coast of Cuba and the atrocities which are ascribed to him are almost incredible. It is said that he frequently threw overboard the crews of ships which he took. He is reported to have struck off with his own arm the heads of ninety prisoners, refreshing himself by sucking the blood as it trickled down his cutlass. It is even related that in transports of frantic cruelty he has been known to pluck out the tongues of his captives and to devour the hearts of those who fell by his hand. By such acts of detestable inhumanity this monster not only gratified his savage nature, but increased his evil powers, for he considered the terror inspired by his name among the best means of promoting his success.'

This, at least, is a danger which cruise passengers do not have to run.

Hot and Cold

When travelling I take a perverse pleasure in quick and extreme changes of temperature. There is an obvious pleasure in flying out of a wet, cold London and leaving the aircraft two or three hours later in bright, warm sunshine. But the pleasure in reversing the process is less obvious. So steep is the climb, by road, from the hot dry plains of Argentina up into high mountain country that one can easily go from a sweltering 90°F. to a shivering 40°F. in two hours of motoring. One of the steepest road ascents accompanied by an equally steep fall in temperature which I have experienced is on the island of Tenerife. In less than an hour you can drive from sea level, temperature 80° or 85°F., to seven thousand feet up the crater slopes of Teyde, with the temperature at about 32°F. We had a disagreeable shock—again there was that perverse satisfaction peculiar to the real traveller—as a result of a flight from Auckland in North Island, New Zealand to Christchurch about an hour away, in South Island. When we left Auckland the thermometer was low in the Fahrenheit nineties; when we landed at Christchurch it was in the low forties. And there, though it was late Spring, it stayed. One of the most gratifying of these violent changes we experienced between Calcutta and Kalimpong. In Calcutta the temperature stood at over 100°F. which is, however, less oppressive there than, for example, in Singapore where humidity is so high; after a flight of about two hours and a drive of an hour, climbing all the time through teak forests and avoiding the monkeys playing in the road, we got out of the car into cold mountain air not much above 40°F.

Drive to Livadia

The drive along the Black Sea corniche road from Yalta to
Livadia is among the most beautiful in the world: deep sapphire
sea, brilliant sunshine, a fascinating Mediterranean-type flora
including cypress and cedar and hibiscus, an endlessly various
and visually pleasing topography, and Italianate palaces set
beautifully among trees. But it was rather marred for us by a
curiously infuriating argument which nearly degenerated into a
row, with our Soviet interpreter, the only disagreeable one we
had during our journey across the Soviet Union. This was a
young woman with so many nervous tics and such a mania for
timing everything we did down to the half minute, that she
clearly needed the attention of a psychiatrist, a profession
which by her own account did not exist in the USSR because
there was no nervous disease. As she told us this while repeatedly
shutting her eyes for half a minute at a time, and wringing her
hands like a Comédie Française actress expressing grief and
despair, we were unconvinced.

However, that was not the subject of the quarrel. We had
asked her to explain to us the workings of the Soviet Health
service, for most of the palaces and new buildings we saw in the
course of the drive were clinics. When she had finished her
explanation I mildly commented that it seemed very like the
British National Health service. She at once became very
excited, shutting her eyes and wringing her hands frantically.
She said that she knew all about our so-called Health Service,
that there was no comparison, that it was not for the Workers,
that it was not free, that in this as in other respects the Workers
in Britain were exploited. Mary said sharply that we might
surely be allowed to know how our own Health Service worked,
and that as she had had her last child 'on' the Service, she could
speak from experience. Our guide's method of dealing with this
was flatly to deny its truth which we perhaps foolishly found

irritating; but she was clearly drawing so close to an hysterical outburst that we broke off the argument.

However, it was a case, with this tiresome young woman, of being between Scylla and Charybdis. For when we asked, by way of half-changing the subject, what diseases were treated and nursed in the scores of clinics we were passing, she could not make up her mind to admit that there were any diseases in the USSR. Were they tuberculosis clinics? Certainly not, tuberculosis had been eliminated in the USSR. Cancer? Cancer was extremely rare in the USSR. Having run through the list, including nervous diseases, with negative results, one of us, probably Mary, wondered aloud that the USSR should need so many clinics where disease had been abolished. Our lady, still with firmly shut eyes and wringing her hands in some kind of moral agony, replied that the clinics were for tired workers to rest in. We dropped the whole subject.

Manners and Latitude

The influence of sunshine and temperature on manners is so marked that in the southern hemisphere it clearly works upside down. The nearer the tropic (but short of it, the tropical zone has its own rules) the more languid, the more genial, the more apt to indulge in *dolce far niente* the people. Of course, one must make reservations; one must discount severe poverty, local climate or other special conditions. And there are gradations; the southern Englishman, a slack and easy-going type, is to the Yorkshireman as the North Italian, who's a sort of Yorkshireman, is to the Neapolitan. Even in the USSR these rules apply, and their working is, in fact, quite striking. In Minsk we found a sort of Russian northcountrymen, full of good will, certainly, but rough and even grim on the surface and with a keen sense of humour which rarely finds expression in smiles. Go to Odessa, Yalta, anywhere in the south, and manners are Italianate—more smiles, more laughter and an attitude to work which is not nearly so glum.

In Australia the relatively sober and energetic Melburnians regard the northerners of Sydney as a lazy, careless lot; and in other parts of the world where the sun is over your right shoulder it is much the same, the bustling and serious southern Patagonians considering the northerners of Argentina, Chile and Peru as loafers spoilt by the sun.

The sun may not be good for the character but it is for the temper.

The Time Lag

A great deal of nonsense is written, talked and broadcast about the famous time-lag fatigue which is supposed to be one of the consequences of long-distance flying. I would guess that the measure of fatigue really due to time-lag disturbance is directly proportional to the subject's degree of belief in the objective validity of temporal mensuration. You leave London at 8 a.m. and when you land in New York your watch says 2 p.m. But the New York clocks show the time as 9 a.m. Adjusting yourself to New York time you go to bed at, say, eleven by your hotel clock, that is 4 a.m. of the next day by your own watch which still shows London time. In short, you have had a long day. But that is all that has happened—no more than staying up till the small hours for a good party. And suppose you allow yourself a long sleep and don't get up till one p.m.—for lunch—by

your own watch, that is get rid of your fatigue by sleeping for
nine hours, it will still be only 8 a.m. New York time, and you'll
have a whole day before you. Why should there be any special
fatigue?

Now take it the other way round. Your flight is from New
York to London. You leave New York at noon by your watch
which by now is set to New York time. At six p.m. by your
watch you arrive in London where Big Ben says that the time is
11 p.m. Deciding to adjust as quickly as possible to London
time you go to bed at Big Ben's midnight. It's only seven p.m.
by your watch but then, when you rise at eight London time
after your usual eight hours sleep, what does it matter that your
watch tells you that in New York it's still only three in the
morning? The time told by a clock is important only to people
who have never realised that there is no such thing in Nature as
an hour or a minute. Only days are 'real' and even then I know
of nothing but habit which says that we humans must regulate
our movements by the sun. Men used to rise with the sun and
go to bed at nightfall principally, like other animals, for want of
light to see by. But night workers who reverse this order suffer
no serious inconvenience. And since we had good artificial light
we have become at least semi-nocturnal—to an extent, indeed,
which is ridiculously wasteful of daylight in high altitudes
during the spring and summer.

Any very long journey is tiring, whether on foot, horseback,
in a car or an aeroplane. Only on board ship is the factor of
fatigue almost eliminated. But even so, the measure of fatigue is,
at least in my experience, largerly a matter of your state of general
health, state of mind, digestion and so on. My longest day's
travel was nineteen hours at the wheel of a car and during the
seventeenth we crossed a high pass by a bad road, in moonlight,
a pass which was supposed to be dangerous at night. Neither of
us was exhausted, or any the worse next day: and the reason is
that we were perfectly well, very happy and enjoying the drive
through magnificent country. When driving on a motorway—

by far the most exhausting kind of driving—when my mind was not at peace and I had indigestion, I have been exhausted to the point of collapse after eight hours.

I do not believe that long distance flying fatigue has much to do with the famous time lag. I do believe that it may be tiring for many people to sit still in one, cramped position for eight, ten, fourteen hours. In short, long distance flying is tiring because airlines are greedy and do not allow passengers enough room; this state of affairs will be improved by the *Concorde*, simply by halving the passengers' term of cramp; but aggravated by the Jumbo jets which will be flown on the cheap.

There is another factor: British people and a majority of Europeans live at or very near sea level, for the most part between one hundred and five hundred feet of altitude. Airliners are pressurized at the equivalent of four thousand feet; it would increase costs and lower profits to pressurize at lower altitude levels. It is probable that for people living at sea level, many hours at 4000 ft. pressure, i.e. in a relatively rarefied atmosphere, is tiring; in a day or two they would, of course, adjust to it; but they do not have time to do so even on the longest trans-Pacific flights.

Another fatigue factor is what I call being mucked about. No large airport in existence has been designed to handle the traffic it is handling: there is the tiresome and often much too long drive to the airport, which could be eliminated by monorail or underground railways; there is the hanging about in crowded, noisy, and in some countries (including England), dirty lounges; there are the humiliating and pointless passport, currency and customs controls (happily minimised now to vanishing point in continental Europe); there is often a long walk on overpolished floors (easily eliminated by moving ways); or the hideously uncomfortable ride in an overcrowded bus to the aircraft.

All these are certainly exhausting: the time lag is not.

Rough Travels

In 1899 David Rough, at that time in his eighties, published a series of accounts of his travels all over the world in the *Dundee Evening Telegraph*. They were subsequently republished by that newspaper as a little book.

Rough was a remarkable man, a true traveller. Beginning with his native town of Dundee, in 1820, he describes his journeys in Russia, India, South-east Asia, Australia, New Zealand; how he fought, as a volunteer, against pirates in the Chatham Islands, visited America in 1844, went to the South Sea Islands, Egypt, Palestine, Greece, Turkey, and all Europe. What were his qualifications as a traveller? Here is a passage which, I think, explains him:

'On our return, as the cholera had appeared in Russia, we had to pass a fortnight in quarantine in the Firth of Forth. On our release the captain had to go on shore on business, taking me as one of his boat's crew. When he came back to the boat, late at night, the men were all away drinking in public houses, so that he and I had to row off to the brig in darkness, much to his vexation and displeasure. When we got on board I overheard him say to the mate, that whenever the boat was sent on shore I was to be sent in her. I mention this proof of his confidence in me because I think it had some good influence on the whole of my after life, for without having any special ability, I have, under Providence, been led to success in filling several appointments of trust both at sea and in public office simply by endeavouring to do the duties of them with faithfulness, and with some amount of zeal, which I would recommend to young men as being the surest way to get on in the world, even when the high mental attainments may be wanting.'

Rough Extracts In Russia (c. 1830)
'At that time the Russian people were contented with the rule of

the Tzar Nicholas, grandfather of the reigning emperor, who did not fear to be seen on foot watching the progress of the work on the Cathedral of St. Isaac, then in course of erection.'

By the time this was written it had become less safe for Tsars to mix with their people. Alexander II had been assassinated in 1881, more or less as a result of the failure of Mr Rough's Nicholas to force reforms on the nobility and gentry.

Of Java in 1835

'. . . the soil is rich and the native people gentle and industrious. The varied scenery of the mountains, valleys, flat lands is very beautiful. In my time there were no railways, but excellent road and well managed posting and post hotels; so that an overland journey, which I made in the year 1835, from Batavia to Samarang and Sourabaya, about 500 miles, was most interesting and delightful.'

We can vouch for Java's beauty still but it is hardly the paradise Rough described while he was staying with the Sultan of Madura. We found Djakarta a slum teeming with miserable beggars, very different from the trim and orderly Batavia of 1835. We stayed in Bogor also, but I have described this elsewhere. The people are gentle certainly, in their manners, and among the most beautiful in the world. In uniform, and led by ambitious generals who swarm like lice on a dog, sucking the life out of the country, they are as ferocious as any other race and shortly before our visit had perpetrated one of the greatest massacres in history.

Sydney in the 1830s

'. . . on the following day we were on the coast of Australia, arriving soon after at the fine harbour of Sydney, so much renowned for safety and for beauty. At that time the convict banishment system was still in force, but soon afterwards was terminated, leaving society very different from what it now is in New South Wales. Hard suspicious feelings seemed to pervade all classes and although many of the convicts had attained positions of great wealth and independence, they were not received into the society of the free colonists. The colony of Victoria and the now great and prosperous city of Melbourne were then of small account, and Queensland almost unknown.' Two things transformed this picture: gold and wool. The second picture, what we saw ourselves in Australia, is being transformed again, this time by the country's newly found mineral wealth.

New Zealand in the 1840s

Rough was in at the making of New Zealand. He sailed from Melbourne to the Bay Islands. The ship carried sheep and cattle for the colony about to be founded and, as their owner fell ill, Rough undertook to look after them:

'It was hard work, for the men in charge were not up to their duties, but it was profitable as well as pleasing to myself to aid in preventing the loss of fine stock as well as money to the proprietor, who was very grateful for my services and paid me the cost of my passage.'

At the Bay of Islands he stayed with the missionaries at the Pahia settlement. He had a letter of introduction to Governor Hobson who took Rough with him to the signing of the Treaty of Waitangi whereby a number of Maori chiefs ceded their authority to Queen Victoria but 'retained their rights of proprietorship in the soil'. He was also present at the founding of Auckland and describes it as follows:

'I was happily able to be of some assistance to Governor Hobson in selecting the best position for a settlement, as far as the harbour and navigation were concerned. We visited the Tamaki River and afterwards the Waitemate, a spacious harbour, well suited for communication with many parts of the country inland. On our return to the Bay of Islands His Excellency, in a very kind and flattering manner, offered me the appointment of Harbourmaster at the Waitemate, where he had determined the seat of Government, to be called Auckland, should be formed. Subsequently a Lieutenant of the Royal Navy came with a recommendation from high authority for his appointment to the office, but the Governor declined to make any change. Soon afterwards the Surveyor-General and myself were despatched and directed to fix the precise spot as most suitable for a settlement, and for a port of easy access and safe anchorage for shipping. We were accompanied by several officers of the Civil Service, and a body of mechanics and working men in a hired transport under my control. Our tents were pitched on a beautiful slope facing the entrance of the harbour, amidst trees adorned with fine paradise plants and hanging clematis flowers. On the 18th September 1840 I had the honour and satisfaction of hoisting the first British flag after Captain W. Symonds, who had been appointed to the office of Resident Magistrate, had procured the necessary land from the natives to be the property of Her Majesty; and the ceremony was concluded by hearty cheers and a salute from the ship. Some weeks later the Governor came from the Bay of Islands in a ship of war, and expressed himself well pleased with the spot selected.'

New Zealand might, in the mid-nineteenth century, have become a part of the U.S.A. had a certain Captain M'Kiver U.S.N., of the man o' war *St. Louis,* been either bolder or less scrupulous. In 1844 the Maoris rose against the British in the new Bay of Islands colony, drove off the garrison, scattered the settlers and burnt the new town of Russel. Chief Heke, the Maori leader, went aboard the *St. Louis* which lay off Russel, and formally asked M'Kiver to take the place for America. The American captain declined and he would not take any part in the fighting between the British troops and the Maoris but promised Heke that he would '... prevent any attempt to injure women and children.' He took many of the Maori women and children on board his ship, but also the British missionaries, which must, in the circumstances, have made a curious ship's company. He took all these refugees to Auckland after landing a supply of ship's biscuit for those British who remained behind. Rough says, 'When leaving Auckland to return to the Bay of Islands he gave me an American flag to be hoisted on any defenceless vessel bearing despatches and requiring protection at the Bay of Islands.'

Rough in Capetown

You visit South Africa and are received with warmth and hospitality. In our case, friends drove us about the Cape, others put a car at our disposal, we were generously entertained to dinner. In spite of this; in spite too of the liberally minded people we met; in spite of the beauty of Table Mountain, and Cape flora, its heaths and proteas and cycads; in spite of the lovely seventeenth and eighteenth century Dutch domestic architecture and nearly perfect climate, South Africa is an unhappy country.

A Sunday morning incident: we were walking through the shopping street of Newlands, the suburb of Cape Town where we were staying. An African woman was trying to restrain two small children who were being normally mischievous. Suddenly with a cry of rage she picked up a large piece of wood from the pavement and threw it at them. She missed the children and we ducked away as it whizzed past missing us very narrowly. The woman stopped shouting and looked at us terror-stricken, cringing and grey-faced. For a moment we were put out; violence, even at that level, is always upsetting; then we walked on. Over our shoulders we saw her hurrying down the street with her now subdued children clinging to her skirts. Our white faces had succeeded where no amount of maternal rage could.

We wished many times that we could enjoy this lovely country, but it was no use. We wished that the Blacks, Whites and Coloured could live together on equal terms as they do in Brazil where the inequalities are the old ones of money not colour, and the class war is not a race war.

David Rough visited Cape Town in 1837, here is his brief description:

'When off the Cape of Good Hope we encountered a heavy westerly gale of wind and high sea. The vessel sprung a leak and we put into Simon's Bay, the naval station of South Africa which is connected to Cape Town by a pleasant road and drive of several hours. At that time South Africa was not much before the public mind and Cape Town was a quiet agreeable place of resort for members of the East Indian Civil Service on furlough. There were no docks or harbour works, only landing jetties and vessels had to ride at anchor in Table Bay, exposed to the fury of sudden storms coming down from the great flat-topped Table Mountain standing behind the town. In fine weather this mountain can be seen from a great distance at sea, long before the lower land comes into view, and it seems to rise above the surface of the water like a stupendous altar which is frequently covered by a table cloth of dark clouds foretelling coming tempests.'

But the evil has always been there for the colony was based on slavery. The slaves were not, it is true, Bantu, for in the seventeenth century the Bantu were slowly migrating into the Cape, like the Dutch themselves. The slaves were Angolans, and Jan van Riebeck, the great founder of the colony has some notes about them in his *Diary*. He says, for instance:

'Guinea and Angola slaves are inclined to desert, especially now that 14 slaves have run away last night from the free-sawyer's Leendert Cornelissen and . . . who treat their slaves better than other freemen do . . .'

We savour the word 'desert'; and wonder how long, even without *apartheid*, it takes to clean away the taint of slavery: five centuries?

Civil Strife

Java is not an island where one feels quite easy in one's mind when there is an appearance of violence about to break out. Any sort of riot or brawl in the streets, anywhere, is alarming; but in, for example, Paris or Rome you feel as a European that you know more or less what its limits will be. Rising early one morning in Djakarta, we became aware of a noisy and threatening commotion in the big square outside our hotel. It began exactly like the cheeping of tens of thousands of starlings going to roost, but, rising in volume and deepening in tone, conveyed the feeling of rage which is only human. Half-dressed we peered out of the windows. An enormous crowd of young people of both sexes was collected in the square, shouting, cheering and chanting. It was contained by a ring of white police jeeps each mounting a machine gun, and as we watched, one of the gun crews opened fire, then another. There was going to be a massacre. At the first burst the people began to run, pouring into the streets leading out of the square, and away down the motorway to the airport, in a dark stream which grew thinner and more straggling as the faster runners outdistanced the slower. Another burst from a police machine gun and the square was clear. But where were the corpses, where the wounded, where the blood? The police had evidently been shooting not at the crowd, but over it.

We dressed, went downstairs and asked a porter what it had all been about. University students had wanted to use the airport motorway, the only decent road near the city, as a motor-racing track; the police objected, the students insisted, and the police had asserted their authority with machine guns. Photographed at the right moment, this farcical non-event could have been represented as a civil riot.

Empty Australia

Australia is the most urban, or maybe one should say suburban, country in the world and the image of Australians as a big open-air type working on a ranch or a farm is misleading. Not that he doesn't exist; he does, but he's rare and nine out of ten Australians are office or factory workers living on the eastern or southern coastal fringe. When you motor inland, as we did, you are at first delighted with the vast emptiness of the land; and then, after a time, and despite your preoccupation with the strange, dry, harsh beauty of a country which has been exceptionally well served and truly conveyed by its painters, you become appalled. This empty wildness in an overcrowded world seems shocking.

There is one sure way of developing country agriculturally: settle peasants on it. At a party in Melbourne one of the guests, a young man, a seventh-generation Australian, showed great affection for Greek music and dancing and spoke of Greece and the Greeks with enthusiasm. Mary suggested that it would be a good idea to settle Greek and southern Italian (she dare not add, Japanese) peasants in some of empty fringe country, on relatively small holdings. Such people would, by their industry and by their passionate attachment to any piece of land they could call their own, steadily push out the limits of fertile country, bringing up the water for irrigation from deep artesian wells.

Our Australian friend became very excited and almost abusive; the very idea upset him. The last thing Australia wanted was laborious peasants; it was, and must remain, a land where a man could be boss of a million acres and live on it without drudgery. The very big holding, worked unintensively, meant the good life.

It is the old *latifundia* idea, of course. In the later years of the Roman Republic the Italian peasantry were dispossessed by

129

its means. One cannot fairly accuse Australia of dispossessing anyone. But the Australians' attachment to the *latifundia* can, perhaps, not unfairly be seen as holding tens of thousands of hardworking south European peasants out of possession of land which they might make something of for themselves and for a world menaced by famine.

Astrology in Ceylon

The Botanic Gardens of Peradeniya on the outskirts of Kandy in Ceylon is one of the most beautiful places we have ever seen anywhere in the world. As I have described it in another book,[1] I shall not do so here. While we were walking along the lovely river walk in the garden, a couple of very beautiful young people got out of an elderly motorcar, the girl wearing one of the most exquisite saris we had seen in all Ceylon and India, and approached us. The young man bowed and asked permission to request a favour. I said, 'Please. Of course.' They wanted one of us to take a photograph, with their camera, a venerable apparatus, of them becoming engaged to be married at eleven twenty-eight A.M. We agreed, of course, but I could not forbear to ask why, having decided to become engaged, they had to go through the ceremony of exchanging rings at a particular moment in time. Because that moment had been found to be propitious by their astrologer without whose advice neither would dream of taking any important step.

I asked what would have happened if their astrologer had advised them against marrying; would his advice have been taken, despite the fact that they loved each other? He *had*

[1] *Great Botanical Gardens of the World.* Nelson, 1969.

130

advised that a marriage between them would not be happy and acting on that advice, and although they were much in love, they had broken off their engagement. But some months later a very eminent Indian astrologer had visited Ceylon and as both of them were very unhappy at being separated they went to consult him, as you or I would consult a medical specialist if dissatisfied with the diagnosis or prescription of a general practitioner. The great man recast their horoscopes and advised that although their own man had not made any mistakes, the prognosis was not necessarily a bad one: he had advised them correctly but their horoscopes could be interpreted more favourably in certain circumstances.

With this encouragement the two young people decided to take a chance and marry.

As well as taking the photograph of their engagement with their own camera, we took some in colour with ours and having been given the young man's address, sent him colour prints from England some weeks later. We received not only a letter of thanks but a charming present, a silver salver with a *repoussé* design of entwined swans.

I should add that both of our Peradeniya acquaintances were university graduates in modern technical disciplines, intelligent, well-educated and, I would guess, well-read.

Puzzle for Sailors

'But he being a man well experienced in the navigation of those seas, bade us all prepare against a storm, which accordingly happened the day following, for a southern wind, called the southern monsoon, began to set in.

'Finding it was like to overblow, we took in our sprit-sail and
stood-by to handle the foresail; but making foul weather we
looked the guns were all fast, and handed the mizzen. The ship
lay very broad off, so we thought it better spooning before the
sea than trying or hulling. We reefed the foresail and set him,
we hauled aft the foresheet; the helm was hard a-weather;
the ship wore bravely. We belayed the fore-down-hall, but the
sail was split, and we hauled down the yard, and got the sail into
the ship, and unbound all the things clear of it. It was a very
fierce storm; the sea broke strange and dangerous. We hauled
off upon the lanyard of the whip-staff, and helped the man at
helm. We would not get down our top-mast, but let all stand,
because she scudded before the sea very well and we knew the
topmast being aloft the ship was the wholesomer and made
better way through the sea, seeing we had sea-room. When the
storm was over we set foresail and mainsail, and brought the ship
to. Then we set the mizzen, maintopsail and foretopsail. Our
course was east-north-east and the starboard tacks aboard, we
cast off our weather-braces and lifts; we set in the lee-braces and
hauled forward by the weather-bowlings, and hauled them
tight, and belayed them, and hauled over the mizzen-tack to
windward, and kept her full and by as near as she would lie.'

Good seamanship? Or a farrago of nonsense? No prizes are
offered. The passage is identified on page 248.

The Temple of the Tooth

No great shrine of a world religion has made less impression on me than the Temple of the Tooth in Kandy. The point, for devout Buddhists, must be in the holiness of the place. The buildings are not unimpressive, but chapel after chapel of identical, enormous and quite unremarkable reclining Buddhas left me uninterested. The orange-robed monks, with their womanly shoulders and arms, shaven heads, hard eyes and ever-open hands—they are the most shameless beggars—are repulsive. Not a trace of the good temper and high-spirited humour we met with in the Hindu temples which are, in any case, artistically far more interesting. I found this visit curiously dispiriting and was left with nothing to say. There was one curious incident, though. To enter the temple precincts you have to remove your shoes. Coming out of the principal body of the temple, we had then to cross a vast gravelled court to see another part of the complex. Charles, our guide, himself a devout Buddhist, put his shoes on and told us we could do likewise to cross the court. About quarter of the way across Charles was accosted by two young men in European clothes who spoke to him in Singhalese. They were obviously very angry about something. I asked Charles what the matter was: the young men objected to our wearing shoes. I at once removed mine and apologised: we had, I said, been told that for crossing the court we were allowed to wear shoes. They moved off with a contemptuous shrug. Charles did not remove his shoes. I asked him why the devil he had told us we could put our shoes on. He said: 'It was only because you're Europeans.'

Nothing could have been less like the courtesy and warmth we met with everywhere in Ceylon and India, but particularly in India. At their best, Indian manners are the best in the world, because with the simple politeness which one meets with in most countries goes a warmth of feeling and a gentle humour, a sort of wry, tacit sharing with you of comic despair over the human condition, which I found utterly charming. Far from disliking the English, Indians seem to prefer us to other Europeans and to Americans. The Americans, of course, have to suffer for being the greatest imperial power on earth; for all men I have met everywhere in the world judge not by facts but by legends, and the legend is that America is wicked, the USSR good; thus Russian imperial dominion over a score of Asian peoples is forgiven or, rather, simply not realised.

But not for a moment did I get the impression that there were Indians who regretted our going. Whereas, in Indonesia, we both—separately—several times got the impression that some Indonesians would have liked to see the Dutch back. One quite considerable man openly said as much, although not where he could be overheard. This so surprised me that when, at Tjibodas, I met a Dutch scientist doing a Unesco job there, I seized a chance, when we were walking alone in open country, to ask him whether he had found any of the Indonesians pro-Dutch. In his fluent but heavy English and with something between a growl and a chuckle, he said, 'At least a bloody sight more pro-Dutch than I am.'

How not to Do It

12 January: 09.00 hours local time. Leave Kalimpong in north-west Bengal, by car, with a Lepcha driver and drive through teak forest, banana plantations and tangerine orchards, in face of strong opposition from monkeys and a long Indian Army convoy driving at fifty miles an hour on an alpine-type road, to Badogra.

12 January, noon. Enplane in a Viscount aircraft and fly to
Calcutta. Drive from Airport to friend's house in Alipore. Bath,
change, collect vast amount of luggage, drive at nightfall to
Airport, fascinated by people whose only dwelling is the street,
cooking the evening meal on various home-made devices.
(Europe, excepting southern Italy, does not know what poverty
means.)

12 January, 21.00 hours. Enplane for Bombay. Stretch legs at
Bombay. Large whisky. Back in the aircraft and off again.

12 January, about midnight. Land at Karachi. Large whisky,
from our own bottle as we found at the admirably stocked Duty
Free Shop that our Indian rupees were refused. Realise we are
in Pakistan. Off again.

13 January. Dawn. Addis Ababa. All our denominations of money
refused, so no whisky and not even coffee.

13 January. Arrive at New Stanley Hotel, Nairobi, having lost
count of time. Actual travelling time, 28 hours. Thank God for
whisky and go to bed.

In the D.D.R.

Perhaps the most unpleasant drive we have done was from the
nasty little town of Hoff in the German Federal Republic to
Berlin by *autobahn*. Those of us who live in freedom are bound
to feel a little nervous in those countries where the politicians—
at their best the basest of men—have got the upper hand of the
people by means of force instead of, as in democracies, by means
of fraud. But neither of us ever felt so uneasy in the USSR or
Yugoslavia, in Spain or Portugal, as in the D.D.R.; and I think
the reason is that the D.D.R. is—or at least was, in 1967—

reminiscent of the most hideous manifestations of the Nation State which has ever been inflicted by the power lust on suffering humanity: Nazi Germany. We were in Hoff by a sort of accident: we reached it, the nearest town to the frontier between the two Germanies, rather late in the evening, were saved by a kindly German who nearly wrecked his car to do us a service, from getting onto the road to Berlin after dark, and decided to spend the night at Hoff and face the D.D.R. ordeal by daylight.

The Hotel Strauss was a sad place. It was not a bad hotel; the rooms were big, the furniture massive nineteenth century stuff, the bedding repaired but of fine quality; it was fairly clean and the dinner was good; and it was very cheap. We were alone in the high, resonant dining-room and in the little bar, after dinner, there was only one depressed commercial traveller. The hotel people were civil and helpful, but we were glad to leave in the morning. We bought a picnic lunch for our 200 kilometre drive in the principal grocery, a sort of small supermarket; and two bottles of beer.

Our trials began at the frontier; I made some kind of mistake in placing the car in the complicated system of metal sheep pens which had been erected to process the motorway traffic, and was sent by a vicious looking juvenile delinquent in Vopo uniform to wait in a penalty pound. Then we were sent to buy transit visas at £1 apiece. There was much form filling to be done. Every official we had to do with was icily polite, as unhelpful as possible, and obviously hated us and each other. They looked poorly clad and poorly fed which probably accounts for their manners.

Next we were told that our international insurance was not valid in the D.D.R. and sent to buy state insurance. The office would not accept our West German marks nor any money but their own. We were sent to another office to buy some and given a rate of exchange which was a crude fraud. By the time it came to our turn to go to the top and have our papers examined by more Vopos or soldiers, openly commanded by a big Russian wearing the uniform of a colonel in the Red Army, the general feeling of being pushed around and hated had made us more nervous than ever. Since our car has right-hand drive I gave Mary the papers to hold as I knew the police would come to her side. There was by then a large sheaf of them and she held them on her lap with her left hand. Presently a young man put his hand into the car on her side for the papers. For some reason— a sort of reflex—Mary shook it cordially and, as we had recently been in Austria, said *'Grüss Gott'*. The officer was so astounded, or perhaps upset by this Christian and sisterly greeting that he blushed all over his face and waved to me to drive on. Perhaps we got him into trouble for being secretly acquainted with a female imperialist.

In the course of a brief hectoring we had received while getting our papers in order we had been told that we must not stop before reaching Berlin, and above all that we must not leave the *autobahn*. We did not propose to take this literally but we drove the first hundred kilometres as fast as we could. There was almost no traffic and I drove at 100 mph. Beside the *autobahn* there are picnic places—a rustic table with benches. We stopped at one of these and unpacked our lunch and our beer. We had hardly started on it when a Vopo Volkswagen drew up and we thought that we were in trouble; our nerves had not been improved in tone by the fact that every footbridge over the motorway was manned by a Vopo with a sub-machine gun. As all these People's Police seem to be jumpy-looking teenagers, the spectacle was not reassuring. But the Vopos in the car did not get out; they simply sat there and stared at us, one of them wearing Tonton Macoute glasses. Maybe they were hoping to be offered a beer and a sandwich; certainly they had a lean and hungry look. As for our appetite, it had vanished. We scrupulously put our rubbish into the bin provided, and drove on. When we crossed the frontier into Berlin we felt suddenly high spirited and excited.

We had a repeat performance on our way out of Berlin to Holland. It may well be that Vopos and D.D.R. bureaucrats are no worse than any other police and officials; and that there is nothing to be afraid of in that Republic. But the place *felt* wrong—not like the USSR, or Yugoslavia or any other communist country we have been in; more like the Germany of the Nazis.

Breakdown in Spain

Driving across the vast plain of central Spain on the way from Cordoba to Badajoz, in the month of August and with the temperature at over 100°F., there was a sharp, fairly loud bang from the car and I could feel that the engine had become disconnected from the wheels. We were ten or twelve miles from the last village, in any case a poor one, and marooned in the middle of an endless plain of stubble, where maize and wheat had been cut.

Beside the road and a score of yards back from it was an open-sided bothy made of bundles of maize stalks and wheat straw, roofed with rough thatch. A tall, lean, yellow-faced man came out of it, accompanied by a boy who appeared to be an idiot. The man asked if something was wrong. I told him that either the clutch or the gear-box was broken and asked where was the next garage. There was, he said, a hamlet three kilometres up the road, with a filling station: perhaps the man there could help. It was, he said, too far for me to walk in the blazing sunshine; he would send the boy, who was used to it. And he very courteously invited us to sit in the shade of his straw hut. He apologised for having nothing to offer us by way of refreshment excepting water, but the water was at least cold.

The shade of his hut was a great relief from the hammer blows of the sun, reddish in a sky hazed by dust. It was furnished with a camp bed covered with grey blankets, a stool and a small, roughly made table. The water chatty was kept under the bed and the water was deliciously cool. Our host was some sort of public game-keeper, and, also from under the bed, came a couple of partridges which he had raised from chicks and which he allowed us to handle. Conversation was restricted by our poor Spanish but we learned that the harvest had been good and that the hamlet he had sent the boy to was a small, poor one.

After less than an hour we saw an old Chevrolet car approaching, with the game warden's boy beside the driver. This driver was a stocky, cheerful man with a nut-brown face and a lot of grey hair forming a bushy fringe below the edges of a tweed cap. I explained, as best I could, what I thought was wrong with the car, and he at once said there was nothing he could do. His advice was to go on to the nearest town of Llerena, seventeen kilometres up the road where there was a workshop which maintained tractors and vehicles for the farmers' cooperative.

'But my car will not go.'

'Then I will tow you.'

Those seventeen kilometres were a nightmare. The tow-rope was short yet the garage man drove at forty miles an hour and every time he checked I nearly crashed into him. He was a very cheerful man, roaring with laughter at every near miss. The temperature inside the car must have been 120°F., and the road was a narrow, raised strip between stubbles and I was afraid that the least mistake would throw us off the road and overturn the car. But we reached that workshop, our friend named his price, I paid it, we shook hands all round and he left us.

The boss of the workshop was a man of thirty, short, sturdy, with black hair and a strong, handsome face. He had that air of assurance and of knowing his job which is so reassuring in

Spanish and Italian master artisans. He had never seen a Citroën DS before. He listened to what I could tell him and then he stationed four of his mechanics—all young boys—round the car, told us to go through all the motions of driving it, and sat beside me as I did so. The car tried to move and one of the boys shouted something. The boss said there was nothing wrong with the clutch or gear-box, the trouble was in the front-wheel drive mechanism of the near-side wheel hub. We had better go to the inn and take rooms for the night and come back in an hour.

The inn was primitive, without running water and with a 'Turkish' lavatory; but it was scrupulously clean and its people were pleasant and welcoming. We installed ourselves, had drinks, and I walked back to the workshop. The sun was declining but there was no evening breeze and the heat radiated by featureless walls would have baked bread. As I have owned cars for forty years and nearly always old ones, I have had much to do with garages and I did not expect any work to have been done. But the hub had been dismantled and its numerous, complicated parts laid orderly on a white sheet. The boss picked up a part, showed me that it was fractured and why it could not be mended. I asked what was to be done. He had ascertained that the nearest Citroën agent was nearly three hundred kilometres away; he could send a car for the spare part. Or one of his mechanics would make a part for me, working all night. We decided on the latter course. On my way back to the inn I began to worry about money. I had not very much and could not get any more until we reached Badajoz.

We were all starving but dinner is not served in Spanish inns, away from the tourist belts, until between ten and eleven. We sat on the terrace with the habitués and as they were all drinking and playing either cards or dominoes, we did likewise. It became cooler and the inn had a cask of ultra-dry, very pale *manzanilla* which we liked. When the dinner came it was excellent and well served.

I was back at the workshop at nine a.m. The work had been finished and the car tested on the road. That is more than a year ago and the car has given no trouble. In trepidation I asked for the bill. I was staggered by it: it was under five pounds. I gave the boy—he was no more—who had made the part on the lathe, a pound. Our bill at the inn for three dinners and two rooms was £1. 14. od.

Many years before the event recounted above I was driving an old but very good Sunbeam car—its date was about 1929— in the Sierra Nevada, and having been brutally forced off the road into a stone-lined ditch by an Hispano-Suiza driven so fast that it was out of control, smashed a universal joint. The car was dragged out of the ditch and to the nearest mountain village by a team of oxen, and as there was, of course, no garage, nor anything of the kind within thirty or forty miles, I myself had to discover what damage had been done. I took the fractured parts of the universal joint to the village blacksmith and after studying them he said he could make one identical with it. But what about the flexible ring, made of guttapercha or something of the kind? The smith suggested that the saddler might help, might make a ring of leather which would at least serve for a few hours' driving. The work done for me by those two crafts- men, and refitted to the car by myself, lasted at least until I changed the car eighteen months later.

USSR Legacies

When it came out a few years ago we enjoyed Pauline de Rothschild's book[1] on her visit to the USSR. There ourselves a couple of years later, we found one difference: Stalin was not made the scapegoat for every past misery and present consequence. I do not mean that the old monster had ceased to be the official scapegoat; but people never mentioned him at all. Like Pauline de Rothschild, we had our surprises. Her guide told her that she and her husband were buying an apartment and that it was costing about $3000, and that the husband's mother was helping them '. . . She inherited some money when my father-in-law died.'

'Inherited?'

'Yes, he was a good engineer and they were well off.'

In our case it was a small country house, a *dacha* which our interlocutor had inherited. I don't know what one imagined happened to a man's private possessions when he died, but we were disconcerted. Inheriting real estate seemed such a very unsocialist custom. At that time Solzhenitsyn's *'Cancer Ward'* and other novels revealing the realities of Soviet society had not yet been published. Now that they have been, one is disappointed, and for a good reason—Pauline de Rothschild rightly says, 'The lack of struggle for money is a privilege in itself, and was in England the very basis of the aristocratic mind and upbringing.' And she quotes something said by Giacometti: 'When I was young I didn't want to have money so as to be free of it. Now I like to have money to be free of it.' There is, in our society, no other way but one had hoped for better things in a socialist society. The new Russian novelists have revealed Soviet society as being much the same as ours: it has been corrupted without ever having been quite pure.

But this is not quite apparent to the foreign visitor partly

[1] *The Irrational Journey*. Hamish Hamilton.

because there is no commercial advertising. It is, ironically, the conversations with Intourist guides which reveal just how bourgeois Soviet society has become. They are so anxious to demonstrate that Soviet citizens, too, have material prosperity that what they show you is the acquisitive society with another face.

I want to quote one other passage from Pauline de Rothschild's book:[1]
'It is curious what a good interpreter makes of you. You become an intense watcher, a listener listening just a little too carefully, the way actors do. Two people, the one who just spoke and the one who will be answering, are watching each other's face. Hardly ever the interpreter's. The one is seeking in the other the reason for the words, their other meaning. This gives the conversation a strange leisure, yet tightens it below the surface. At least in Russia.'

Soviet Intourist interpreters are astonishingly good. Ludmilla, our very charming guide in Minsk, was outstanding. I had to carry on a long conversation with the Director of the botanic garden there, one of the best in the USSR, a conversation full of technicalities and spotted with botanical Latin. She was not once at fault. But she did better than simply convey the meaning of each to the other. She was quick to sense that Dr. N. V. Smolsky and I found each other *sympathique*, and she somehow made herself the interpreter of our warmth as well as of our words. Because of her our time at Minsk, not intrinsically a pleasant place, was one of the happiest parts of our stay in the Soviets.

In Tashkent, Uzbekistan, where I had to see and talk with the Academician Rusanov, we had a different kind of interpreter. Full of good will but unable to cope with the technicalities, he tried improvising, causing a confusion resolved, in the event, by the common ground of botanical Latin. But that was

[1] *The Irrational Journey*. Hamish Hamilton.

not all; the interpreter, knowing nothing of botany or horti-
culture, was seized by a new curiosity and passion to learn; you
could see that he was surprised to find all this so interesting.
Too interesting, for he began to neglect his duty as interpreter
to ask questions on his own account; and but for Rusanov's very
powerful personality and, in the end, firmness, the occasion
would have turned into a Russian comedy.

On one occasion, this time in South America, we had a really
bad interpreter. I had to deliver a lecture to quite a large
audience at the San Martin theatre in Buenos Aires. As my
remnant of Spanish is not nearly good enough for lecturing,
I was to talk in English which was all right because most of my
audience understood it. But as it was thought that about a
quarter of them did not, my lecture was to be translated into
Spanish as it proceeded, the interpreter sitting at my side and
sharing the microphone. Listening to his translation I soon
realised that he understood only about half of what I was saying
and was *ad libbing* in such a way as to make a nonsense of a good
deal of it. I was trying to bring myself to the point of protesting
to my Chairman when one of the many bilingual members of the
audience stood up and did it for me; as he was immediately
supported from all over the theatre, the poor interpreter was too
embarrassed to defend himself and for the rest of the lecture only
translated a sentence now and again, when he was quite sure
what I meant.

The Blue Circuit

There is a peculiar satisfaction in driving through a string of famous place-names. For some it is the names of battles: in Moscow we met a party of French people whose tour of one of the most extraordinary countries in the world was, if you please, confined to Napoleon's battlefields. If you like Champagne, or at least its glamour, try the Blue Circuit round the *Côtes des Noirs* of the so-called Mountain of Rheims. The names you will drive through are Verzy, Verzenay, Beaumont, Mailly, Rilly, Sillery, Trepail, Villers-Marmery, Ludes, Chigny-les-Roses, Villers-Allerand, Chamery, Ecueil, Sacy, Villedommage, Jorny, Parguy. There are also the Red and the Green champagne circuits, the red being the *Côtes de Bouzy et d'Amboise*, and the green the *Côtes des Blancs*.

Durocortorum

That was the Roman name for Rheims. In his admirable *The French Vineyards* (Eyre & Spottiswoode), Mr Denis Morris says:

'The old Roman caves have a much greater depth than more recent, commercial excavations. The former are the quarries from which the Romans took enormous blocks for use in building, for repairs and ramparts. Being somewhat more cultivated than those who desecrate our modern countryside by inflicting deep wounds on large surfaces, they quarried intelligently, making their excavations in the form of pyramids, which yielded an enormous amount of material without affecting the surface. Standing at the bottom of one of these pyramids, as I did with M. Jean Marc Heidsieck, you can just see a Dutchman's trouser patch of light some 150 feet above. Around you rest hundreds of thousands of bottles of champagne . . .'

Wine Rivers

The great vineyards of France were planted, where possible, near rivers for a very good reason: the only way to get the wine out to distant markets was by boats. The three greatest wine rivers in the world are—with due respect to the Saône—the Garonne, the Dordogne and the Isle, all of which become the Gironde at Bordeaux. By a happy coincidence the country they flow through is lovely in its variety, its diversity of charm, and its range. It includes mountains, with the dramatic and exciting gorges of the Tarn which is a tributary of the Garonne; rich farmland worked nowadays with tractors although one still sees teams of oxen; soft and gentle hills, great forests; pinelands and sandy flats and a fine sea coast. Above all there are the rivers themselves, sometimes slow and deep and stately, at others rushing turbulent over shallow, rocky beds, or tumbling noisily through narrow gorges and over rapids. The land of the Dordogne is particularly beautiful. There are the Lascaux caves with their treasure, the earliest works of artistic genius by European man. This country has a magnificent flora, with whole fields of narcissus in spring and in summer an abundance of Lizard Orchids, the most curious and spectacular of the European wild orchids.

The Garonne, with its two sources, one in the Roussillon and one in the Jurançon, flows between the ancient counties of Gaillac and Armagnac with their old stone towns and fragments of castellated walls; through the Sauternes and Barsac country —five *communes* of great wine châteaux—the most famous of these being Château d'Yquem.

Another wine country, the *Entre-Deux-Mers* used to grow sweet white wines but is now making them dry. The two '*mers*' it lies '*entre*' are, of course, not seas but the Garonne and the Dordogne. And on the other bank of the Garonne is the Graves country and beyond it, on a great inlet of the sea, the holiday centre of Arcachon, and the great salt mere, the Etang de Lacanau with its hundreds of thousands of wild fowl. Graves has 43 wine-growing *communes*: one thinks of Graves wines as white; but the two greatest, Haut-Brion, and La Mission Haut-Brion, are reds. The latter château, a very handsome one, has been overtaken by the sprawling suburbs of Bordeaux.

It is beyond the city that the three rivers flow as one and become the Gironde. This flows by way of Haut Médoc and Médoc to the sea. The Médoc *communes* include Margaux, St. Julien, St. Estèphe and Pauillac, the *communes* of the world's greatest red wines with such names as Lafite, Latour and Margaux, Montrose and Cos d'Estournel and a dozen others.

If you return south-west from the Médoc, back to Bordeaux, across the river and the middle of the Entre-Deux-Mers triangle and carry on up and over the Dordogne at Libourne, you will be in Claret country again. Follow the Dordogne valley to Bergerac, a pleasant town, quiet and complacent. The upper reaches of the valley are honeycombed with caves, including the painted caves of Lascaux and Les Eyzies; Lascaux, of course, is now closed to visitors. This is all fine walking country, with orchids and asphodel, tiny ancient villages and the golden Montbazillac wine.

If you make another turn, back to Les Eyzies and go north through the truffle town, Périgueux, through Mussidan to Contras, between Contras and Libourne, in the tip of the triangle formed by the Dordogne and the Isle, is more wine country, Pomerol. To the east lies St. Emilion and, across the Isle, the Côtes de Blaye.

The Third Wine River

From Nantes to Angers, Tours and Orleans is about the most fatly satisfying, and in places loveliest, countryside in Europe, including Britain. This, of course, is the 'Château country' and the long rosary of castles and great houses is threaded on the Loire, each dominating some gentle, or glorious, or spectacular view of plump alluvial farmland, hill, woods, vineyards and river meadows.

If we count the Dordogne–Garonne–Isle complex as viti-culturally or oinologically one river, and call the Saône the second wine river of France, then the Loire is the third. The first clear mention of wine-growing in its valley does not occur until Merovingian times, but then in such terms that it is clear that the vineyards had been established for many generations.

Gregory of Tours, bishop of that city, has much to say about Loire viticulture in his *History of the Franks*: there are vine-yards throughout his diocese; damage to the grapes by bad autumn weather is a public calamity. But what is very curious, Gregory describes how year after year during the reigns of Kings Chilric, Gontran and Childebert II, the Bretons raided Nantes, centre of the Loire wine trade, seized and held the vineyards, picked the grapes, pressed them, and retreated back into Brittany carrying the new wine with them.

The wine lands you travel through if you follow the Loire are four. But the first, near the source, is in the Jura and its wines are not really Loire wines at all. So beginning in the west, you are in *Muscadet* country. The wine named *Muscadet* derives not from a country but from a vine variety—*Muscadet de Bourgogne*. Next along the river comes Anjou, and then Vouvray. But as well as these three, the Loire has lesser wine regions—Saumur for example, Sancerre, Pouilly-fumé and Bourgueil.

For the traveller the whole valley is pleasant going, with almost as much to see as to drink: we remember the lovely ducal palace of Nantes and the fine Gothic cathedral, the charm of Saumur and Vouvray, the exquisite beauty of the countryside between Nantes and Angers, the 14th century tapestry in Angers castle, the pretty villages of the Touraine, the cave dwellings in the Loire cliffs, to say nothing of the châteaux themselves.

The Use of Rage

No quality is more necessary to the traveller than patience and the power to keep one's temper. But it can be immensely exhilarating on very rare occasions to lose one's temper completely; it can even—but again very rarely—get results which calm and patience fail to get. We were trying to fly from Nairobi to Cape Town but were having the greatest difficulty in getting onto a flight as far as Johannesburg where we had a firm booking for a certain date and time. We managed it at last, checked in Johannesburg and registered our luggage and then had an hour or two to wait. When we presented ourselves at the specified time we found that the airline had heavily overbooked the flight and that there were no seats for us—and about fifteen other equally indignant people. Protests, ticket-shaking and demanding to see a higher authority were all met with Afrikaner stolidity and the implied answer that shouting and abuse would not stretch the aeroplane; and a promise of seats on the first flight next morning. Defeated, I asked for our luggage back. Impossible: it had already been loaded into the aeroplane and could not possibly be unloaded.

That was the word which suddenly released in me the divine afflatus of the kind of rage which seems to make even a mild man terrifying. 'Unauthorized' persons are not, of course, allowed to go marching out onto the tarmac of airports. I am, eminently, an unauthorized person. But possessed by rage, authority descended upon me. I seized a uniformed and astounded young woman by the arm, and using her uniform as a passport marched her out to the aeroplane, and demanded our luggage from the hold, by that time nearly fully loaded. The captain of the plane was there. He refused to unload and ordered me off the tarmac. I told him that he could either take us or that I would stay there till I got all four cases out. He saw the fire of the kind of anger burning in me which makes a man wholly un-amenable to any pressure short of force; and with a furious gesture he ordered the black porters (who enjoyed this disgrace-ful scene enormously) to unload the hold and get our luggage out.

This was a victory I could enjoy. For the ordinary, mild, reasonable man, victorious rage over another individual is followed by shame. But nobody need be ashamed of defeating the obstructiveness and punishing the inefficiency of a great commercial company or state institution.

Arabian Medicine

One of the few places in the world which has not yet been rationalized is Oman and what remains of the older Arabia. Dr. Wendell Phillips, oil tycoon and archaeologist writes:
'In the former Aden Protectorates the tying of a thin black goat hair cord around the upper part of the calf of the leg is considered an infallible insurance against snake bite, while in Yemen a string tied around the big toe prevents rheumatism,

and a raven's intestines, if administered in an agreeable form, are considered vital to improving a child's memorizing powers. There is scarcely one Arab in a hundred in all the Arabian Peninsula who has not some cautery scars on his body, for the hot iron is accounted the universal panacea for man and beast in Arabia, the underlying idea perhaps being to create an extreme counter-irritation which becomes a festering sore. Even infants are burned cruelly. A hot iron over the spleen is prescribed for malaria and one at the base of the skull for boils. In bad cases of consumption the bottom of the tongue is branded, causing it to swell, filling the mouth with unbelievable agony so that the patient cannot speak or eat. A popular Hadhrami cure for acute abdominal pain is the deep burning of the patient's heel with a red-hot iron stake. The shock effect alone usually succeeds and the sufferer exchanges his stomach ache for a ten-day limp. If the hot iron fails, the Arab resorts to written words from the Quran, which the patient takes by swallowing, paper and all, or by drinking water in which the ink of the writing has been dissolved. In most of these instances the patient is armed with one or several popular amulets or shields consisting of a chapter or verse from the Quran folded in a small leather case and hung on the person. Babies are adorned with charms which not only serve to keep off the evil-eye, but are amusing playthings. In addition, old teeth, coins, holy earth and beads are used, as well as the spittle of a holy men applied to the ailing organ of the body. This sure protection and guardian from the excessively dreaded influence of the evil-eye (blue eyes are particularly nefarious) is applied as well to camels, horses, donkeys, houses and fishing-boats. For here sickness is due to the hand of God or the evil-eye which is ever going to and fro to discover its prey. "It empties the houses and fills the tombs." More than half of all deaths are attributed to the evil-eye, which must somehow be misled, deceived and deluded and its effect dissipated.'

Other Places, Other Ways

This was told to me by Dr. Wendell Phillips, whose travels in Oman have been extensive. Sheikh Salim bin Diyan of the Bani Kaab tribe had been saying his prayers one Friday in the mosque at Mahdha. As he rose to his feet his brother Maadid shot him dead through one of the mosque windows. Murder is not considered a crime against the tribe, i.e. against society, but only against the murdered man's family, and the penalty is a payment of blood-money to the victim's next-of-kin. The Bani Kaab accepted Maadid as their Sheikh; his murder had been a crime against God, as well as against himself as Salim's kinsman; but that was his business. It seems that there was nothing remarkable about this: assassination did not exclude the assassin from Sheikhdom, and in what used to be the Aden Protectorates a sheikh was always more or less in danger of being assassinated by the man who was to, and did, succeed him.

'May Allah show mercy to the tongues of travellers.'

Hold up

Driving through the central mountains of Sicily, on fairly difficult roads through magnificent country with a fascinating flora, we realised, after some time, that we were being followed; or at all events that there was a FIAT, with four men behind us. As I have always enjoyed fast driving on alpine roads, I decided to shake the other car off. But it was useless; the driver of the FIAT behind us was at least as good as I am and despite our front-wheel drive lost only a few yards on the corners.

At last Mary asked me to let him pass, and on a short straight I slowed and the FIAT overtook us. From the back seat one of the four men in it was waving something at us. I said he wanted us to stop: Mary said, 'Don't'. Tracing back the reason for a certain nervousness: in the hotel at Agrigento we had taken a certain table on the café terrace; a group of three men, all in very respectable black suits and black hats, came and stood over us. There were other tables unoccupied, but there they stood, saying nothing, just . . . impending. The pressure exerted by their patient silence was extraordinary; and presently we got up, moved to another table, and they sat at ours. *Maffiosi*. That was their table. And who were we to defy the real government of Sicily?

The FIAT stopped; the two men in the back seat got out. One of them held up a red-circled white disc on a stick. I pulled up. We waited. They came to the door of the car. 'Good afternoon, *polizzia*.' 'Good afternoon, gentlemen.' Were we French? No, English. Where were we going? Gela. Did we like Sicily? Oh very much, it was the most beautiful island in the world. They beamed; we beamed. They warned us with kindly warmth that the road ahead of us was atrocious and that we should be careful; they turned out to be as the Australians say, too right. We exchanged farewells, they left us, drove on; and presently we followed; but slowly.

Roman France

Provence was, of course, the oldest Gallic province of the Roman Empire, a highly civilized Greek colony when Rome was a cattle-herdsmen's squalid village. This is apparent in its build-

ings, the arenas at Arles and Orange, the Maison Carrée in
Nîmes, the forum in Orange, and the aqueduct called the Pont
du Gard, one of the most moving of ancient buildings, presumably because of its dramatic setting and appearance and its
social significance. The amphitheatres in Arles and Orange are
still in use. Late in July there is a drama festival at Orange and
some of the best companies in France are to be seen there,
notably the Comédie Française. Since Roman engineers, copy-
ing their Greek mentors, had mastered the technicalities of
acoustics, the Orange amphitheatre is the best open air theatre
I have ever visited.

Daudet's Mill

Of the Provence towns Tarascon comes nearest to confirming
Alphonse Daudet's idea of that country. What about Avignon,
better known to us because of the song? Yes, well, it is a matter
of taste. Of course, the great *Palais des Papes*, towering above
the Rhône valley, should be visited and its tremendous view
enjoyed; and there is the bridge, reaching half-way across the
river where *L'on y danse, l'on y chante* . . . But it is a glaring,
dusty, noisy, harsh place, whereas Tarascon is quiet, well
shaded, dreaming and good natured: but only on the surface.
Daudet's Tartarin of Tarascon is, in my opinion, a crashing
bore, and I don't believe in him: he is a product of self-
conscious literary regionalism. There is nothing mild or comic
about Provence; it is tough and bitter. I visited—God knows
why—the famous mill where Daudet wrote *Lettres de mon
Moulin* and that archly whimsical *La Mule du Pape*. The mill is
now a literary shrine and I had a long talk with its *gardien*. He

knew and cared nothing about Alphonse Daudet, reciting his piece about the author parrot-wise. But he was a considerable expert on Charles Dickens and talked most interestingly about him.

Travel Ad.

Leaving New York at midnight in high spirits—being bound for Nice and an encounter I was looking forward to with all my heart—and atrocious weather. Pouring rain, a kind of fog, and a gusting gale at Kennedy Airport. The aeroplane was a new mark—the Super VC 10. Weather notwithstanding it took off in time and for some minutes was bucketing about as aeroplanes used to do in the old days when they had airscrews. To soothe our alarm the Captain came on the P.A. system: he apologised for the discomfort; very shortly we should be comfortable, he was climbing to get above the weather. Presently we levelled off and everything was still and calm. I ordered a double whisky and marvelled at the quietness of this, incomparably the most comfortable aeroplane of its 'generation'. And I was not the only one to appreciate the qualities of that beautiful machine: the Captain addressed us again. 'We are now flying at . . .' some hardly credible altitude . . ., 'and our air-speed is . . .' some scarcely believable velocity; 'and passengers may be interested to know that our rivals the Boeings are still being bounced up and down by the storm five thousand feet below us . . .'

Clavijo in Samarkand

In 1404 a Spanish gentleman, Clavijo by name, went as Ambassador from the King of Castille and Leon to the Great Khan, Timur (Tamburlaine), whose court was in Samarkand. Timur, who was seventy at the time and almost blind, granted the Spaniard an audience. Clavijo described it as follows:

'We came to a great orchard with a palace therein, a considerable distance outside the city. Attendants there took charge of us, holding each ambassador under the armpit, and led us forward, entering the orchard by a wide and very high gateway, most beautifully decorated with tiles in gold and blue. We came to a certain great lord of the court, a very old man, seated on a raised dais, and we all made him a reverence. Passing on we came before another dais where we found seated several young princes, His Highness's grandsons, to whom also we paid our respects.

'Coming next to the presence beyond, we found Timur seated under what might be called a portal before the entrance to a most beautiful palace. He was seated not on the ground but on a raised dais with a fountain before it which threw up water into the air, backwards, and in its basin were floating red apples. His Highness had taken his place on what appeared to be a small mattress stuffed thick and covered with embroidered silk, and he was leaning on his elbow against some round cushions piled behind him. He was dressed in a plain, unembroidered silk cloak, and wore on his head a tall white hat on whose crown was displayed a ruby.'

Timur was a great maker of very great gardens and Clavijo was lodged in a pavilion in one of them. Everything he saw astonished him and no doubt it was all very splendid by comparison with the squalor of mediaeval Spain. He was particularly fascinated by the huge silk tents, erected by the Mongols for their magnificent garden parties.

'It was four square in shape. In height it was the measure of
three long lances such as are used by a horse-soldier, and the
side was a hundred paces from angle to angle. The ceiling of the
pavilion was made circular to form a dome and the poles supporting it were twelve in number each as thick round as the
chest of a man breast high. These poles were painted in colors
blue and gold and otherwise, and of these twelve great tent
poles four were placed at the corners with two others in between
on the side. Each pole was made up of three lengths which were
firmly joined together to form the whole. When they had to be
set up the work people made use of a windlass . . . From each
of these poles at its summit on the dome-shaped ceiling there
hangs one end of a great curtain in silk cloth that is thereto
attached, and these likewise form a square, and above they join
to the tent wall of the pavilion. The outer tent walls of the four
porticos . . . are supported by twenty-four small wooden
masts . . . and the structure is stayed by upwards of five
hundred ropes, and these are colored red.

'The exterior walls of the pavilion are made of a silk cloth
woven in bands of white and black and yellow. Outside at each
corner is set a very tall staff capped with an apple of burnished
copper above which is a crescent. The summit of the pavilion is
square shaped with four tall staves at the corners, each with its
apple and crescent. The staves are set at a great height and they
form the framework of what is like a turret made of silk cloth
set with what simulates battlements. There is a gangway from
below to come up into the turret . . . to repair the faults. It is a
wonder to behold and magnificent beyond description.'

Ancient Roads

So important is travel as an element of civilization that a State which builds no roads cannot be called civilized. Among the most remarkable road systems in pre-technical times was that in the Incas of ancient pre-Conquest Peru. The roads were engineered to minimise gradients and were paved with flat stones. As the ancient South Americans had no riding animals and no vehicles—indeed, they had not even the wheel—the roads were only six feet wide. the 'mails' were carried by runners, relaying each other, the stages being one mile apart. Post runners were expected to sprint their mile and were given a ration of *coca* (from which we derive cocaine) as a stimulant. A message was carried from source to destination at an average speed of 6 mph, but in an emergency 12 mph was attained. At the time of the Spanish conquest the principal high roads went north from Quito, south through Caxamarca, Cuzco and other cities to fork at Titicaca, one branch going north-east round the lake of that name into what is now north-west Argentina, the other down to the Chilean coast to join up with the lowland system which, linking the extreme north to the extreme south of the Empire, extended over 2,000 miles. Where necessary tunnels were driven through hills; and bridges able to bear an army on the march or a herd of llamas moving to new pasture were thrown across rivers and gorges. These were suspension bridges of maguey fibre spun into stout ropes, slung from stone pillars. There were five of these cables, the three lower ones being boarded over, the other two serving as rails. Some of these bridges were as much as seventy yards long and lasted, with frequent cable renewal by skilled bridge-keepers whose national service, in the Inca communist system, this was, well into the nineteenth century, long after the Empire had fallen to dust.

The first Europeans to travel over some of these roads were

Pizarro's men. Pizarro while on the march to Caxamarca where he had learnt that the Sapa Inca Atahualpa—a usurper, by the way, his brother and prisoner Huascar was the rightful Sapa Inca—had his court and was taking the baths, had one of his officers, De Soto, sent with a detachment to spy out the land. De Soto visited two cities, Caxas and Huancabamba. The houses he found built of dressed stone and he describes the high road as paved with stone and shaded by regularly planted *molle* and willow-trees. Such evidences of civilization greatly worried the Spaniards as they travelled towards Caxamarca. When they first sighted the town they were even more disconcerted. Of straw-coloured adobe and pale grey limestone, it was 'like a sparkling gem in the dark skirts of the *sierra*.' And before that gem, as if to guard it, was Atahualpa's army, encamped:

'It filled us with amazement to behold the Indians occupying so proud a position. So many tents so well appointed as were never seen in the Indies till now. The spectacle caused confusion and something like fear in the stoutest hearts.'

Venice and Tenochtitlan

The charm of Venice, its well-deserved fame for beauty, is not simply in the fact that it is built in water—water which is inexorably rising to drown it—but lies also in the grace of its palaces. But, then, they to a considerable extent owe their beauty to having been built to rise out of the water which mirrors them, so that, of course, we get back to water as the principal aesthetic element in the Venetian scene.

I know of only one other city ever built, like Venice, in water, and with canals for streets: Mexico-Tenochtitlan, the great city built in a lake by the Aztecs. The old centre of the city was a rock on which was built the tenochtli, the house of god, i.e. the national temple of Uizilopochtli. Around it the lake shore swept in a curve strung with villages. South of the salt lake—Texcoco —were the fresh-water lakes Xochimilcho and Chalco. There were swamps, sandbanks, inlets—a land and water mixture. This, with almost incredible perseverance and ingenuity, the Aztecs, by digging canals and piling up dikes and building on piles, built into a great and beautiful city. It was planned and built as a square, the new (sixteenth century) roads on the grid system, with canals instead of streets, and paths on the earth banks beside them. It covered 2,500 acres.

A fair estimate of the population of this Central American Venice, at the time of the Spanish Conquest, based on Cortes' estimate of the number of houses—one hundred thousand—is seven hundred thousand. It was certainly not less than half a million or as great as one million. The population of our Venice is about three hundred and seventy thousand.

The chronicler Bernal Diaz says that when the Spaniards saw Mexico they saw 'things unseen, nor ever dreamed.' Cortes himself describes the houses as beautiful, though it can hardly have been with the beauty of Venetian palaces. There were both flat and hanging gardens which he much admired, parallel canals and streets, and a busy traffic of boats on the canals.

The Emperor Montezuma II himself took Cortes to the top of the principal *teocalhi* temple pyramid—one hundred and fourteen steps to the top—to show him the city. 'And' says Diaz del Castillo:

'told him to look at the great city and all the other towns near by on the lake and the many villages on the dry land . . . This great accursed temple was so high that from the top of it everything could be seen perfectly. And from up there we saw the three causeways that lead into Mexico—the causeway of Iztapalapan, by which we had come four days earlier; the causeway of

Tlacopan, by which we were later to flee, on the night of our great defeat . . . and that of Tepeyacac. We saw the aqueduct that comes from Chapultepec to supply the town with sweet water, and at intervals along the three causeways the bridges which let the water flow from one part of the lake to another. We saw a multitude of boats upon the great lake, some coming with provisions, some going off loaded with Merchandise . . . and in these towns we saw temples and oratories shaped like towers and bastions, all shining white, a wonderful thing to behold. And we saw the terraced houses, and along the causeways other towers and chapels that looked like fortresses. So, having gazed at all this and reflected upon it, we turned our eyes to the great market place and the host of people down there who were buying and selling: the hum and the murmur of their voices could have been heard for more than a league. And among us were soldiers who had been in many parts of the world, at Constantinople, all over Italy, and at Rome; and they said they had never seen a market so well ordered, so large and so crowded with people.'

The Spaniards destroyed Mexico-Tenochtitlan. The sea is destroying Venice; surely nobody will ever build a city of canals again.

City Remembrances

Cities are supposed to be remembered for architectural features, or perhaps for one outstanding monument. But it is not always so. What stands clear in our memory of Sydney, for example, is first the beautiful topography of the city: as in San Francisco, it's the shape of the city under one's feet that stays in the mind.

That, and the streets of nineteenth-century houses with their pretty cast-iron work in the balconies, rather than the spectacular Opera House. And the reason for this seeming perversity of memory is obvious: photography has made every famous building in the world familiar long before you see it; it is the lesser features of a town, which you discover for yourself, that become, in memory, the symbol of that town. And that symbol can be an odd one; only in San Francisco, for example, did I ever feel vertigo merely walking the steep streets: vertigo, rather than the city's beauty or the eccentricity of its cable cars, is its symbol. Nairobi and Kampala we shall remember always by the word 'bouganvillea'. A very familiar plant, but not as it is grown there, decorating street after street with garlands, trees, thickets and boskages of flaming colour—all the yellows and oranges and reds and purples.

Markets

Among the pleasures of travel are markets. The best I have ever seen is the street market of La Spezia, in northern Italy. On the appropriate day of the week—I have forgotten which it is—several of the town's broad streets are given over to it. All kinds of goods are sold—clothes, furnishings, shoes, china and cutlery—as well as food, plants and flowers. Once I saw, laid out on the road, a dinner service I wanted, but I did not know whether one accepted the merchant's price, or bargained. Most people seemed to be bargaining. Buying seeds at a seed stall, I discovered that the young woman who kept it spoke English, had lived in England, and was anxious to hear news of Streatham, a place she was fond of. I asked her advice about the dinner service and was told that I should bargain. I said that I did not know how to and she offered to teach me. I think her rules apply not only to Italian street markets but to street markets everywhere excepting, I suppose, in England. The seeds-woman bought the dinner service for me, by way of an object lesson. One should never deprecate the goods in order to lower the price; you praise the goods, you do not hide the fact that you want them, but you confess that the fact is, they are too dear for you, you cannot afford their perfectly fair price and will have to forego the pleasure of owning them. It is then up to the merchant, if he is in fact willing to reduce the price, to say that he would hate to see you disappointed, that it would be a pity you should go without something you want so much for the sake of a few thousand lire; and to lower his price. If it is still not low enough for you, you confess that the most you can afford—it is clearly not enough but you wish to make your position clear—is so-much.

French provincial street markets used to be good and enter-taining but since the introduction of powerful amplifiers to re-inforce the cries of salesmen calling their wares, have become so hideously noisy that one now avoids them. In absolute contrast are Mexican markets, conducted with the quiet dignity peculiar to most American 'Indians'.

The most exotic markets I have seen are Indian. The *Hat* in Kalimpong used to be famous; Sikkhimese and Tibetan caravans reached it, even from across the Himalayas. It is still fascinating, teeming with Sherpa, Lepcha, Buthanese and Tibetans. And it is singularly gay; people of Mongol stock seem to have a very ready sense of humour, shouting witticisms, digging each other in the ribs and roaring with laughter on the slightest occasion. The women selling knitwear, which is remarkably hairy, sit knitting their goods as they mind the stock, and transform selling you a sweater into a comic turn.

Of all the markets I like fish-markets and flower markets best, and for the same reason—pleasure in forms, colours and smells.

The famous flower market at Nice is disappointing: it is over-dominated by carnations. It used to be pleasant to have a bowl of onion soup and a glass of wine at Les Halles in Paris at three or four in the morning; but the market has been moved out onto the Orly motorway and Les Halles are half dead now. But there is, in Paris, a charming little market not nearly well enough known to visitors, the plant-nursery market on the Ile de la Cité, near Notre Dame. Partly in the open, and partly covered, and with the busy Seine on one side, its stall holders deal only in young trees and shrubs and other plants for gardens; pot and house plants, often very exotic ones; and decorative evergreens. It is fresh, and sweet-smelling and tranquil, a delightful corner.

Architectural Note

There is, of course, no such thing as a bogus building. There can be no law which confines a style to the epoch of its invention or to a particular place. Nevertheless, to paraphrase Orwell, some buildings are more authentic than others, more in place and time. Or perhaps one should say no more than that some buildings succeed as works of art and others fail. Of modern buildings three which I have seen seem to me exceptionally successful as works of art: the Museo de Anthropologia in Mexico City; the Museum of Modern Art in Rio de Janeiro; and the Sydney Opera House which looks for all the world like a flotilla of lateen-rigged sailing boats on the waters of that great Harbour. For an example of a world famous building which is not a work of art, here is the late Aldous Huxley's account of the Taj Mahal:

'. . . we drove out to have our first look at the marvel by the light of the setting sun. Nature did its best for the Taj. The west was duly red, and orange, and yellow, and, finally, emerald green, grading into pale and flawless blue towards the zenith. Two evening stars, Venus and Mercury, pursued the sunken sun. The sacred Jumna was like a sheet of silver between its banks. Beyond it the plains stretched greyly away into the vapours of distance. The gardens were rich with turf, with cypresses, palms, and peepul trees, with long shadows and rosy lights, with the noise of grasshoppers, the calling of enormous owls, the indefatigable hammering of a coppersmith bird. Nature, I repeat, did its best. But though it adorned, it could not improve the works of man. The Taj, even at sunset, even reverberated upside down from tanks and river, even in conjunction with melancholy cypresses—the Taj was a disappointment.

'My failure to appreciate the Taj is due, I think, to the fact that, while I am very fond of architecture and the decorative arts, I am very little interested in the expensive or the picturesque, as such and by themselves. Now the great qualities of the Taj are precisely those of expensiveness and picturesqueness. Milk-white amongst its dark cypresses, flawlessly mirrored, it is positively the *Toteninsel* of Arnold Boeklin come true. And its costliness is fabulous. Its marbles are carved and filigreed, are patterned with an inlay of precious stones. The smallest rose or poppy on the royal tombs is an affair of twenty or thirty cornelians, onyxes, agates, chrysolites. The New Jerusalem was not more rich in variety of precious pebbles . . . .

'This inordinate costliness is what most people seem to like about the Taj. And if they are disappointed with it (I have met several who were, and always for the same reason) it is because the building is not quite so expensive as they thought it was. Clambering among the roofs they have found evidence to show that the marble is only a veneer over cheaper masonry, not solid.

It is a swindle! Meanwhile the guides and guardians are earning their money by insisting on the Taj's costliness. 'All marble,' they say, 'all precious stones.' They want you to touch as well as look, to realise the richness not with the eyes alone, but intimately with the fingers. I have seen guides in Europe doing the same. Expensiveness is everywhere admired . . .'[1]

Huxley, of course, was exceptionally endowed for forming his own judgements and dared to point out that the four minarets of the Taj are 'among the ugliest structures ever erected by human hands.' And bearing out his argument that too many people are impressed by mere expensiveness, he dwelt on the fact that the artistic superiority of London's St. Paul's Cathedral over Rome's St. Peter's is commonly overlooked because St. Peter's is of marble, St. Paul's of Portland stone. The superior beauty of St. Paul's has been made a great deal more manifest by the cleaning of the building which, of course, Huxley never saw.

Sacred Cows

Of all travels writers Aldous Huxley kept his head best, levelly judging what he saw, and not only on the matter of architecture. He is the antithesis of the too credulous and respectful Herodotus. When we were in Calcutta we were very disgusted to see the damage done by sacred cows to very poor people; and the lamentable condition of the cows themselves. On the bridge which leads into the atrocious suburb of Howrah, a place of indescribable and indescribably squalid poverty, we saw one of these wretched animals eat the half-dozen lettuces on which,

[1] *Jesting Pilate.* Collected Works. Chatto & Windus, London. 1957.

no doubt, the poor devil offering them for sale depended for that day's living. The animals are always raiding greengrocery shops and stalls in that way. Now, here is Huxley in Srinagar: 'Srinagar owns a large population of sacred cows and bulls that wander vaguely through the streets, picking up such vegetable garbage, grass and fallen leaves as they can find. They are small beasts—the half of good-sized English cattle—and marvellously mild. Red rags mean nothing to these little bulls, they can be trusted in china shops—even in nurseries. Liberty, underfeeding, and unlimited access to the females of their species account, no doubt, for this surprising gentleness.

'But, though harmless, these Hindu totems are passively a nuisance. They will not attack you as you walk or drive along the streets, but neither will they get out of your way. They stand there, meditatively ruminating, in the middle of the road, and no shouting, no ringing of bells or hooting of horns will send them away. Not until you are right on top of them will they move. The fact is, of course, that they know their own sacredness. They have learned by long experience that they can stand in the road as much as they like and that, however furiously the klaxon sounds, nothing will ever happen to them. Nothing: for Kashmir, although its inhabitants are mostly Mohammedans, is ruled by a pious Hindu dynasty. Up till a few years ago a man who killed a cow was sentenced to death. Under a milder dispensation he now gets only a matter of seven years penal servitude. A salutary fear of cows is rooted in the breast of every Kashmiri chauffeur. And the totems know it. With a majestic impertinence they stroll along the middle of the roads. When one is a god, one does not disturb oneself for the convenience of mere man, however importunate.

'To the eye of pure reason there is something singularly illogical about the way in which the Hindus shrink from killing cows or eating their flesh when dead, but have no scruples about making the life of the sacred beasts, by their ill-treatment, a hell on earth. So strict is the orthodoxy of Kashmir, that Bovril is confiscated at the frontier, and sportsmen are forbidden to shoot the wild *Nilgai*, which is not bovine at all, but happens to be miscalled the 'blue cow'; the very name is sacred. And yet nothing is done to protect these god-like animals from any cruelty that does not actually result in death. They are under-fed and, when used as draft animals, mercilessly overdriven. When the goad fails to make them move, their driver will seize them by the tail and, going through the motions of one who tries to start up a Ford car, violently twists. In winter, when fodder runs short, the Kashmiris pack their beasts together in a confined space until they begin to sweat, then turn them out into the snow, in the hope that they will catch pneumonia and die. To the eye of reason, I repeat it, it certainly seems strange. But then the majority of human actions are not meant to be looked at with the eye of reason.[1]

Birds

We are not ornithologists and do not actually know that, of the fifty odd countries we have travelled in, Australia and Mexico are richest in birds. Probably it just seemed like that to us. In south and central America generally the humming-birds are a delight; the commonplace cliché, winged jewels, alone describes them; and yet it is very unsatisfactory for what is most striking about them is their vibrant energy, their vivid success in making visible the exquisite play of forces in balance. In no form of life is the attribute 'life' made so exquisitely and elegantly manifest. At the other extreme of the size scale are Mexico's turkeys and vultures—*zopilote*; one kind of *zopilote* is

[1] *Jesting Pilate*, Huxley, Aldous. Chatto & Windus. Collected Works, 1957.

not much bigger than a farmyard chicken; the other is as big as a turkey. The turkeys you see in Mexico now are, it seems, no longer wild, though I don't think they are actually extinct in the wild. In Australia we never got used to the stupid way in which the *galahs*—grey and pink parrots as big as crows, refuse to take off from the road as you approach in your car, until the very last moment. Time and again we nearly killed one. Nor did we get used to the gaudy colours of Australian birds, especially the bright emerald green of flocks of small parrots.

Marvels

You travel to see marvels and you see them, whether of art or nature. But marvels don't last. It is of the essence of the marvellous that it be incredible, and therefore believed in only by an act of faith. No work of art or architecture, however sublime, can remain a marvel once thoroughly seen and studied; it is revealed as a product of logic, however eccentric. The revelation brings with it a deeper, maturer pleasure, displacing the simpler delight of wonder. Two works, but of nature, retain for me their marvellous quality: the enormous blue and almond green butterflies of Brazil; and a plant, the Jade Vine, *Strongylodon macrobotrys*, which we first saw in the Botanic Garden in Singapore.

There are, of course, innumerable other creatures, animal or vegetable, whose exquisite forms and colours, whose living geometry, seem unaccountable for by any refinement of natural selection; whose attributes of shape, colour or device seem altogether excessive for their purpose—survival; seem, therefore, combined, composed for pleasure only, even at the cost of viability. I do not know why the two creatures I have named leave me still merely—well, wondering. For others, there will be some other natural phenomena which remain indigestible by reason, suspended in the limbo of marvels.

No plant can surely, *need*—to maintain the species—a hanging two- or three-foot inflorescence of three-inch flowers, shaped like a lobster-claw and coloured an electric jade green?

Kittens

The young Kikuyu who drove us through the small but exciting game reserve near Nairobi—so near that patrons of the local drive-in cinema complain of lions jumping the fence to see the movies—was very good indeed at his job. It is delightful to see splendid animals at their ease in natural surroundings. We saw herds of wildebeeste, zebra, ostrich, giraffe; we saw a lioness. All the animals simply ignore motor-cars, but react at once if someone gets out of his car.

In a stretch of open, brown grass, with only one small clump of trees, our driver stopped suddenly, staring. He pointed; we could see nothing. He eased the car nearer, and slowly nearer to whatever creature he had spotted. When he stopped again, we saw her—but only her head: a crouched cheetah. We were, I suppose, ten yards away from her. We sat staring at her, she away from us with that extraordinary air of indifference common to all the cats. We were about to drive on when the cheetah suddenly stood up and, in the same instant was surrounded by five delightful cubs, silvery grey, unspotted and silky; and bursting and bouncing with joyous excitement. It is for such moments that one travels.

Back in Nairobi we were envied; it was known that a cheetah in the park had been seen with five cubs, but only by a ranger.

And so ridiculous are our kind, we felt extremely proud of ourselves, as if we, not the cheetah, had made that litter of kittens.

The Proud Corrupt

One of the oddest manifestations of human behaviour is pride in what is nothing to be proud of. People in countries where corruption is on a grand scale—most 'emergent' African countries, most Arab countries, Iran—tell you about the latest fraudulent conversion scandel with as much pride as if they were boasting of some great national achievement in the arts, sciences, or at least sport. Duncan Forbes wrote:[1]

'Teheran talks cynically about corruption as we grumble about the weather. Frequently even pride seems to glint in their eyes as some scandal involving public transport or fisheries or building contracts or land tenure is revealed.'

It is a good analogue because we, that is the English, certainly take pride in the sheer badness of our weather. And Mr Forbes says, too:

'One met people with relatives in jail, but no personal stigma seemed to attach to their imprisonment. They were regarded as having had bad luck . . .'

We met with precisely the same manifestation in other countries, although, perhaps, for corruption Iran can have no rival, since virtually all the money received in foreign aid vanished into private bank accounts without altering the condition of the people in any way. Americans recount their appalling violent crime statistics with pride: it is as important and gratify-

[1] *The Heart of Iran.* Hale, London. 1963.

ing to them that more people are murdered per annum in such-
and-such a city than in all Europe, as that such-and-such a
building is the tallest in the world. Singhalese urge you to deal
in currency on the black market. Indians are vastly amused at
the way in which a certain Bengali merchant got a consignment
of American-aid grain into his hands, and sold it at an enormous
profit to his starving countrymen. Argentinos tell you, with
delight, how a certain famous banking house is defeating some
futile, government effort to better the condition of the people.
My only very rich Italian acquaintance takes the pride of an
artist in a masterpiece in explaining how he swindles the
income tax man; as do my rich American and occasionally
English friends.

I enjoy very much this paragraph from Mr. Forbes' book—
again the country is Iran:

'As a former President of the National Bank said, "Social and
political unrest is a manifestation of the despair and lack of
faith of the people, of their distrust of incompetent and sometimes corrupt governments. It is a challenge which must be
met."'

The gentleman in question was later arrested for squandering
American Aid funds. His bail was set at £50 million.

Apartheid

At Johannesburg Airport, having no South African money, I
tipped a black porter who had handled our considerable luggage
for us, in East African money, explaining that I had nothing
else and that he could change it at the airport bank. An hour
later the porter found me—he had been waiting at the door of

the bar: 'Please, mister, change this money.' The bank had
refused to change it. I took it from him, told him to follow me to
the bank, put the money on the counter and said, 'Change this
into South African money, please.' The clerk did so and I
handed the money to the porter. I said, 'Why wouldn't you do as
much for this man?' The clerk shrugged.

Volterra

Of Tuscany's numberless charms none is more characteristic
than her hill towns. In most of the countrysides of the most
civilized landscape in the world, they are a feature. Sited high,
often walled and fortified, they were safer from marauders than
if they had been built in the plains. The plan of all such towns
is much the same: a level piazza with the *duomo*, that is the
church; across the piazza, the local municipal or regional
government building, the *palazzo communale* or *palazzo del
ragione*. Nearby is likely to be a big stone tank fed by a pipe or
aqueduct from some higher, wooded point in the hills. The
piazza is paved with stone, often, as in Siena and many other
hill towns, laid in a pattern. Mingled with the meaner houses
of piazzas and streets, usually of stone but sometimes of rose-red
brick, there will be one or two Renaissance palaces with carved
doorways and window-frames.

   Volterra is the most impressive hill town in Tuscany, as
Macaulay realised with his

> 'From lordly Volaterra
> Where scowls the far-famed hold
> Piled by the hands of giants
> For God-like kings of old.'

You approach the hill either from Poggibonsi, or from San Gimigiano through olive groves and mulberry plantations, the mulberry trees festooned with high-trained vines which, in autumn, fall into swags under their heavy load of grapes. Stony banks are stippled pink and white with the flowers of *Cyclamen neapolitanum* which, as you get higher, is replaced by heather under fine stands of evergreen oak and sweet chestnut. Either way the last ascent is a long spiral round the hill to the grim, majestic town of the Etruscans, refortified by Siena in her wars with Florence, and the fortress enlarged when Lorenzo dei Medici appropriated the town.

But its prehistory is even more interesting than its history. Velathri of the Etruscans, it was founded in the ninth century BC, and was a great industrial city of bronze- and iron-age workers, miners and quarryers in the metalliferous hills south of the city. This first epoch in the city's history is summed up in the admirable Etruscan Museum in the via Don Minzoni.

Orvieto

If Volterra be the most impressive of Italy's numerous hill towns, there are others pleasanter. Orvieto is a favourite with us. To reach it you turn off the autostrada, climb dizzily zig-zag for twenty minutes or so and emerge almost abruptly in the piazza of one of Italy's prettiest—the word is chosen deliberately— cathedrals.

But the town is much older than Christianity. As Volsinii it was one of twelve cities of the Etruscan Federation, and apparently centred on a temple complex. It was the Etruscans who planted the first vineyards of Orvieto, including Montefiascone away to the west, whose fortune was remade in the middle ages by the wine called Est Est Est. The story they tell you to account for this name is that when Bishop Johannes, of the great Augsburg banking firm of Fugger, was on his way to Rome, he kept a servant riding half a day in front of him to write, on the gates of the towns he passed through EST (It is) if the wine was good; EST EST if it was very good. At Montefiascone he wrote EST EST EST. Johannes Fugger is buried there.

The Romans took and looted Orvieto in 265 BC and Pliny says that they carried away, presumably from temples and mausoleums, two thousand statues. The Etruscan cities to Rome's north had quite as much to do with civilizing the Romans, as did the Greek cities to the south of her. And Orvieto's museums, her private collections, even some of her churches are rich in artefacts of the great Etruscan past.

There is hardly a building in this enchanting hill town which is not either interesting or beautiful; two are outstanding: the 13th century Palazzo del Popolo, with its immense arches, grand staircase and beautiful three-light windows. The stone is golden in the sunshine; and in the spectacle of the busy, cheerful piazza, used as a morning food market, there is a marvellous feeling of the continuity of civilized living during nearly three thousand years. The other superlative monument is the cathedral.

Pope Nicholas IV began to build it in 1290; but that it should be built was decreed by Urban IV who was in Orvieto when, about twenty-four years earlier, a travelling Bohemian priest who had doubts about the miracle of transubstantiation, was vouchsafed a miracle while he was celebrating mass in Bolsena: as he held up the host he saw that it was bleeding and the blood stained the sacrament linen. Knowing that the Holy Father was in Orvieto, the priest hastened there, confessed his sinful doubts, produced proofs of the miracle. Thomas Aquinas was in the town at the same time; perhaps he, too, had a voice in the decision to build a great church.

The cathedral, whose principal architect and artist was the Sienese, Lorenzo Maritani, is at once simpler and more completely a work of art than Siena's, to which it is likened, Its principal glory is the carving of its four marble piers. Garlanded by vines are scenes from both Testaments in bas-relief, from Genesis on the first pier to a grim Last Judgement on the fourth. In all the great body of western Christian art, the façade of Orvieto's basilica is one of the masterpieces.

Siena

When Remus was slain, his son Senus fled north, accompanied by his brother. They were pursued but one of the gods clearly intended them to get clear away, for twice at critical moments they were hidden by clouds, the first black, the second white. When he came to the hill of Siena, Senus set up the Roman wolf and built a city and for his and the city's shield used black-and-white stripes by way of thanks for the same clouds. The pattern is repeated in the alternating black and white marbles in the *Duomo*.

The prosperity of this hill town was founded on wool, Siena's first spinners and weavers being Milanese refugees fleeing from the Emperor Barbarossa's German barbarians in the middle of the twelfth century. It was this trade which first brought the city into competition, resulting in centuries of warfare, with Florence. But it was in money-lending, banking, that the Sienese came to excel, the greatest of the merchant banking families being the Chigi who at one time had over a hundred branches and a fleet of over a hundred merchantmen; moreover, they handled the Vatican account. The city's artisans excelled in working iron and in ceramics.

Few things in history are more extraordinary than the way in which the Italian cities combined progress in all the arts, sciences and refinements of civilization and teaching all Europe the art of living, with almost continuous brawling at home and war abroad. Shakespeare's Montagues and Capulets in Verona are true symbols. In Siena, as even now you will learn if you will listen, the leading families, Saraceni and Marescotti, Chigi and Malavolti, and Piccolomini, Tolomei and Salinbeni were at complex feud, and street-fighting was a daily commonplace. Yet neither the power to improve in the practice of the arts and crafts, sciences and commerce seems to have been impaired, nor the power to wage war with Florence which war, again, seems rather to have stimulated than hindered such progress.

In 1260, when Florence threatened to destroy Siena and the Sienese unless they threw down their walls and laid the city open to Florentine dominion, the city council elected Buonguida Lucari as dictator, dedicated their city to the Virgin—whence its soubriquet *Civitas Virginis*—and, aided by a force of German mercenaries sent by Manfred of Sicily (Siena was as Ghibeline as Florence was Guelf), inflicted a crushing defeat on a numerically superior Florentine army.

The distinguishing feature of Siena is Il Campo, and the distinguishing annual event, the Palio. This vast open space was a field of mud or dust until it was bricked over in the 15th century. It was used for games, tournaments, feasts, races. And there the Palio is held. The best description of it known to me is in Lilian Notestein's *Hill Towns of Italy*.[1]

'This Palio is ostensibly in honour of the Virgin. On the banner (*palio*) awarded to the winning *contrada* on July 2 is a figure of our Lady of Provenzano, on August 16 a depiction of the Assumption. To give the occasion further religious significance the horse of each contestant is led, in advance, into the church of its quarter to be blessed by the priest.

'Only ten of the existing *contrade* are allowed to enter the race.

[1] *Hill Towns of Italy* by Lilian Notestein, Hutchinson, 1963.

For days before, the preparations go on in a tumult of expectation. Each district decorates its streets and buildings with its colors and emblems. There is the wolf, of course, the goose, the eagle, the snail, the turtle, the mussel, the panther, the porcupine, the ram, the owl, the giraffe, the unicorn, the dragon, the caterpillar, the forest with a rhinoceros, the wave with its dolphin, the elephant bearing a tower on its back. Then the flag throwers are rehearsed, two for each *contrada*, and a drummer. They are dressed in medieval costume from the feather in the hat to the pointed shoes. They are as Aldous Huxley says, like 'personages out of a Pinturicchio fresco'.[1] Their flags, each of several colours, they pass back and forth, shift from hand to hand, now under a leg, now over the head, then they hurl them high into the air and catch them as they flutter down.

'During the race, three times around the course, the jockeys urge on their horses by every means available. (One doubts whether they have found any means more efficacious than that medieval one mentioned by Sacchetti of putting a thistle under the tail of the horse.) After it is over, there ensues a night of bacchanalian revel. Forgetting all restraints, men have been known to dive into fountains filled for the occasion with wine.'

Anti-Traveller

'It was then that I left Paris on my longed-for tour of the cities of Europe. It was going to travel! I travelled. Thirty-four times, in haste, panting, I packed and unpacked my trunk. Eleven times I spent a whole day in a train-coach, smothered in dust

[1] *Along the Road*. Huxley, Aldous. Chatto & Windus, (London 1948)

and smoke, suffocating, and jumping off at every stop to gulp miserable lemonades which upset my stomach. Fourteen times I made back-breaking ascents of endless stairways in unknown hotels in the wake of a porter or waiter; looked round me in a strange bedroom; and lost my bearings in a strange bed, from which I awoke to ask, in a strange tongue, for coffee and milk which always tasted to me like broad-beans; and to take a bath in a tub which always smelt of mud. Eight times I had brawls in the street with coachmen who swindled me of my money. I lost a hat-box, fifteen handkerchiefs, three pairs of drawers, two boots, one brown, one patent leather, and both belonging to the right foot. At more than thirty little round tables did I wait disconsolately till they brought me my *boeuf-á-la-mode*, cold, with gravy coagulated; and more than thirty times the wine-waiter brought the Bordeaux which I no sooner tasted than I rejected in disgust. I wandered, in the fresh twilight of granites and marbles, with reverent, muffled steps through twenty-nine cathedrals. I softly trod, with a dull pain in my neck, through fourteen museums, covered all over even to their ceilings with Christs, heroes, saints, nymphs, sombre stains of bitumen, and the infinite sadness of immobile forms! . . . The most pleasing day was when, at Venice, where it poured cats and dogs, I met an old Englishman with a red nose, who used to live at Oporto and knew Ricardo, Jose Duarte, the Viscount of Bon Successo and the Limas of Boã Vista. I spent six thousand francs. I had travelled.'

Eça de Queiros.
The City and the Mountain.

Conversation Pieces

Walking down Southampton Row, my friend the late James
Cleugh was approached by two short, stout, bald and be-
spectacled German tourists.

'Blease, vhere gan ve vind bleasure?'

I meet my friend at the airport of the island where he has come
to join us for a holiday:

Me: Did you bring your driving licence, so you can take your
turn at the wheel?

He: My dear Edward, of course. If you have a heart-attack in
the mountains, I want to be able to get back to the hotel.

Edward Lear, on board ship for India; and a German fellow
traveller:

German: You vear spegtakles always?

E.L.: Yes.

German: They vill all grak in India: von pair is no use.

E.L.: But I have many.

German: How many?

E.L.: Twenty or thirty.

German: It is no good:—they vill all grak:—You should have
got of silver.

E.L.: But I have several of silver.

German: Dat is no use;—they vill rust. You might got gold.

E.L.: But I have some of gold.

German: Dat is more worse: gold is always stealing.

The dialogue is from Lear's *Indian Journal*.

Don Eduardo, as we leave the birthday party for the first
birthday of his eighth child, on our way to one of his ranches:
'I must apologise for the servants you will find there. They are

Chileans. Wretchedly poor people, yet the woman is carrying
her seventh child.'
Myself: 'How very improvident.'
Eduardo: '*Claro.* They are animals.'

The same Don Eduardo, showing us the family photograph
album:
'My grandfather. He had a herd of Jersey cows. For his chest.
Whenever he travelled to Europe, he took always his own cow
with him.'

1938. My first crossing to America.
Scene: The upper deck of the *Queen Mary.*
I am approached by a total stranger who resembles Benito
Mussolini in a black wig.

'Sir, my name is Mordecai Berkmanns. Your face represents
culture.'

Since when I have travelled by air.

And for French-speakers only:

My English friend:	Voulez-vous nous indiquer la route à Albi.
1st peasant:	Albi? Connais-pas.
M.E.F.:	Oui, Albi. C'est tout près.
1st p. to 2nd:	Tu connais, toi?
2nd p.:	Moi? Albi? Non. Et pourtant j'suis du pays, moi.
M.E.F.:	Albi, Albi, Albi ...
1st peasant:	Ah! Al*bi*! Mais, monsieur, il fallait le dire!

The Villa Lante

Of Italy's countless superlative works of art, the garden of the Villa Lante, near Viterbo, is one of the most beautiful I have seen while travelling between Milan in the north and Messina in the south. It was laid out about 1566 by the architect Vignola for Cardinal Gambara. And of this masterpiece that excellent judge Sacheverell Sitwell wrote—'were I to choose the most lovely place of the physical beauty of nature in all Italy, or in all the world that I have seen with my own eyes, I would name the gardens of the Villa Lante.'

At the gate as you go in there is a magnificent Pegasus prancing, surrounded by water-nymphs, in a great pool, by Giambologna. The formal garden is surrounded by a *barco*, a park richly planted with trees. You must go to the high terrace to get the best view of the formal garden; and especially of the square lake, set in golden stone, with its glorious central fountain of four ephebes holding aloft the arms of Cardinal Montalto, a later owner of the villa, surmounted by a star of jets of water; and its pretty stone boats. The upper and lower terraces are linked by a fanciful and altogether enchanting cascade, the *cordonato*, which is in the form of an elongated crayfish—*gambero*—part of Cardinal Gambara's arms. Nor are these all the waterworks, for one of the terraces has a splendid dolphin-and-masks fountain in a stone almost the colour of bronze, so nearly so indeed that I at first took this fountain to be made of bronze. All this and more, a harmony of stone and water, is shaded by magnificent evergreen trees.

On one terrace I remember an open-air dining room, that is a stone table with a channel down the centre for a small stream of water for cooling wine, with stone benches. This must have been copied from the one described by the younger Pliny, which he had at his villa in Tuscany.

The lake is surrounded by four formal parterres of *ricami*—

evergreens clipped in a simple pattern of sweet curves, like embroidery.

No place I have seen anywhere in the world has quite the serene and brooding beauty of this work of garden art. Feeling this same quality, Sacheverell Sitwell tried to explain it: 'All you can say when considering a work of art (Villa Lante is as much a work of art as any poem, painting, piece of music) is that some portion of the weight of aesthetic comes from the other souls that have attached themselves to it in admiration.'

Lear on Malta and Corfu

'I could not live on Malta, there is hardly a bit of green in the whole island—and hot sand stone, walls and bright white houses are all you can see from the highest places, excepting little stupid trees here and there like rubbishy bits of black worsted. The harbours are very interesting, but I don't love the water well enough to portray such scenes characteristically. The street scenery, so bright, so clear, so balconied, is really beautiful—but there the charm ends.'
—and on Corfu
'—lo! all the hedges and trees have said to each other—"bless us"—"here is April the 10th there is no time to lose", and out they have all come in full leaf most wonderfully!—and as for flowers, things have now reached their utmost and I suppose, there is now no more possible room for any more—There is hardly any green left since an immense crop of marigolds, geraniums, orchises, irises and cannonilla have come out. The hills are positively an immense crop of geraniums all gold colour—and in the olive woods the large white heath looks

like snow, and the pale lilac asphodels in such profusion as seen like a pale veil over the ground. The hedges are *absolutely* pink, and in fact the whole is almost absurd from its very oddity.'

These passages are from letters which Lear wrote to his sister Ann, published by Vivien Noakes in her biography of Edward Lear. As a traveller he recorded what he saw more vividly in paintings than in words; yet as a travel writer his touch was intimate and sometimes vivid. Here he is on the subject of Palaeokastrizza which he found utterly peaceful,

'excepting only a dim hum of myriad ripples 500 feet below me. On my left is the convent of Palaeokastrizza and happily, as the monkery had functions at 2 a.m., they are all fast asleep now. To my left is one of the many peacock-tail-hued bays here, reflecting the vast red cliffs and far above them—higher and higher, the immense rock of St. Angelo rising into the air, on whose summit the old castle still is seen a ruin, just 1400 feet above the water. It half seems to me that such life as this must be wholly another from the drum-beating bothery frivolity of the town of Corfu, and I seem to grow a year younger every hour . . .'

And here, on the same place, is a much better writer, Lawrence Durrell:

'Last and most likely is Paleokastrizza, drenched in the silver of olives on the north-western coast. The little bay lies in a trance, drugged with its own extraordinary perfection—a conspiracy of light, air, blue sea, and cypresses. The rock faces splinter the light and reflect it both upward and downward: so that, staring through the broken dazzle of the Ionian sun, the quiet bather in his boat can at the same time look down into three fathoms of water with neither rock nor weed to interrupt the play of the imagination: so that, diving, he may imagine himself breaching the very floor of space itself, until his fingers touch the heavy lush sand: so that, rising to the surface borne upward by air and muscle he feels that it is not only the blue sky that he breaks open with his arms, but the very ceiling of heaven. Here are the grottoes. Paleokratizza has two of them, one reachable by boat and beautiful. The walls are twisted painfully out of volcanic muscle, blood-red, purple, green, and nacreous. A place for resolutions and the meetings of those whose love is timid and undeclared.'

Corfiote Cricket and Brazilian Soccer

Corfu is an island which stimulates dreams. And I don't mean recalling Odysseus and Nausicaa. Watching small boys playing the sort of cricket one used to see in the London slums, with wicket and bails chalked on a wall, and an improvised bat, set off a story that will never be written, of an English ex-officer, a keen cricketer, returning to Corfu, seizing upon the boys' love of the game taught to their grandfathers a century ago by British troops, when all those islands were part of the Empire; secretly creating a Test Team; challenging and beating the West Indies, India, South Africa, England and, finally and perhaps disastrously for Helleno-Australian relations, Australia—with an all-Greek eleven.

And is it so far-fetched? From our waterfront hotel in Rio de Janeiro we could see a dozen soccer fields, some very simple— just the chalked pitch and the goal-posts; others elaborate, with arc-lights enabling the clubs to play until midnight, which some of them did. There were times when we could see half a dozen games played with passionate enthusiasm all at the same time, some by bare-foot, bare-torsoed boys, others by men of League quality, correctly booted and jerseyed despite the heat. It was, I think, a year Brazil won the World Cup. Not so long ago it would not have been any more far-fetched to imagine the exotic heirs of tropical forest tribesmen, Portuguese colonists,

Calabrian and Greek immigrants and African slaves, welded into a new people by a displaced European empire, and an uneasy Republic—beating Britain at soccer, than to imagine Corfu winning what used to be called The Ashes.

But the soccer we saw from our window in Rio had a difference: drum bands whose rhythms either set the pace of the game, or took their pace from it, we could never be sure which. As a goal shot became possible, the drums became frantic, and this quickening, louder, shriller rhythm clearly helped the man with the ball.

Maybe if the Corfiotes ever field a cricket team, it will have a bouzouki band; it would probably be more helpful at the bowling than at the batting end.

Repton's Recipe

In terms of mileage the great landscape gardeners of the eighteenth and nineteenth centuries were necessarily among the greatest travellers of their age. With contracts in execution in great houses as far apart as Yorkshire and Devonshire, they were continuously on the road for days. Humphry Repton rode or drove as far as 500 miles in one week. Early in his life he made a whimsical experiment in the technique of travel, which by his own account stood him in good stead for the rest of his life; he gives an account of it in his only non-technical book, *Odd Whims and Miscellanies*. Repton and three friends set out on a journey 'through the drear sands of Westphalia' and all four travellers indulged the right to complain with what he calls 'all the virulence of English prejudice'. Horses, inns, weather, food, servants, everything is vile. But they found this so depressing to their own spirits that on their second night at an inn the travellers resolved that

'... everyone should affect to be most pleased when he was really most disgusted, and that no one should utter a complaint under the penalty of defraying the day's expenses. By being thus accustomed to be pleasant under difficulties and to laugh at hardships instead of complaining, we became satisfied with our accommodation and in good humour with one another. Indeed so much reason had I to be pleased with its effect, that I determined as far as possible to follow the same cheerful habit in my journey through life; and when disappointment or misfortune have attempted to assail me, I can smile at their attack and call them blessings ...'

Yet travel was his death: having undertaken to escort his daughters to a ball at a nearby country house to his own, and the weather turning to snow, the Reptons' carriage overturned during the drive home in the small hours and, although the girls were unhurt, Humphry received injuries which confined him to a wheelchair for the rest of his life and which were at the last the death of him.

His acquaintance and fellow architect Wyatt was killed in the same way; and it is a fact that carriage travel was not as safe as, in our time, it seems that its ten miles an hour should have been.

At sea in 1402 A.D.

Eye-witness accounts of sea voyages at the end of the 14th and beginning of the 15th century are not common. In 1402 the Norman knight Jean de Bethencourt set out to conquer the Canary Islands (we have referred elsewhere in this volume to his predecessor Lancelot Malocello). An account of the adventures of Bethencourt and his men was kept by his chaplains Pierre Bontier and Jean Le Verrier. Here is a taste of their matter and manner, in my own translation:

'And the Lord of Bethencourt, with him being Messire Gadifer de la Salle and other Gentlemen came to Corunna and there found a Scottish earl, and the Lord of Hely, and Messire Rasse of Renty, and several others, with their troops. Here M. of Bethencourt went ashore and into town where he had business to transact, and found the earl's people stripping a ship which had been taken, we know not from whom. Seeing which Bethencourt asked the earl if he might take from the ship some things which might be of use to us, which the earl granted. And Bethencourt went to the ship and had an anchor and a boat taken, and had them sent to his own ship. But when the Lord of Hely and his companions heard of this they were much displeased. And Messire Rasse of Renty came to us and said that it was not the Lord of Hely's pleasure that our people take the boat or the anchor. Bethencourt answered that it was the Earl of Craforde's (? Crawford) will and that he would not send them back. When the Lord of Hely heard this answer, he came to my Lord of Bethencourt and told him that he must fetch or send back what he had taken from their ship; and he answered that what he had done was by the earl's leave, and they had high words. Thereupon my Lord of Bethencourt said to the Lord of Hely, Take boat and anchor, by God, and be off. Not so, if you please, answered the Lord of Hely, let them be sent back this day, or I shall take other steps. Bethencourt and Gadifer answered him, Take them if you will, we have other things to do. The said Bethencourt was on the point of sailing and about to raise the anchor and move out of the harbour, and so immediately he did.

'When they saw this they manned a boat and followed Bethencourt, but got only within hailing distance, and many words were exchanged which it would be tedious to relate.'

This row may however have been the cause of difficulties which Bethencourt ran into at Seville's Port St. Mary where on the complaint of some English and Genoese merchants he was arrested for piracy. The Royal Council, nevertheless, released him promptly. It seems likely that the pirate in those waters, who had been taking English and Genoese merchant-men, was the Earl of Crawford.

Earthquake

So peculiar and disturbing are even the minor symptons of a small earthquake that even in the absence of spectacular effects it is impossible to be in any doubt about what is happening. Although neither of us had ever been in an earthquake before, when at 1 a.m. on March 1st 1969, we were awakened by a strange juddering of the whole parador where we were staying in Santa Cruz de la Palma, and by a high-pitched, whining vibration of the window-panes, we instantly knew that this was an earthquake. The epicentre was nine hundred miles out in the Atlantic and the quake did no damage where we were.

A lasting kind of damage done by earthquakes is to the beauty of old towns which may be completely wiped out. We were in Tashkent in Uzbekistan, in 1968: it is today a city of great tall blocks of flats, scores of them. Nothing is left of the ancient Tashkent. It was completely wiped out in the earthquake of 1963; loss of life was very light—about 15 people, but more than quarter of a million were unhoused. The new city is doubtless pleasanter, or at least more comfortable, for the poor to live in, but it is not pretty.

Earthquake

Yet, because of the way it was built, it was one of the most impressive things we saw in the USSR. Every sister Republic in the Union sent aid to Uzbekistan not in the form of money but in that of building materials and labour. The builders camped on the site and remained until they had completed their contribution. The smallest and poorest Republic built one block of flats; the richest, Great Russia (Moscow), built a whole complex. The homeless were all rehoused in three years. For the first time hundreds of thousands of Uzbekis saw men of all nations of the Union; and all working to help them. Although there was an overall plan, the style of each building or complex had something characteristic of the Republic which built it. This should have made the new residential quarter of Tashkent lively to look at. But modern Soviet architecture, although not as atrocious as that of the 'thirties, is without grace or distinction.

Edward Lear in his *Journals of a Landscape Painter in Southern Calabria*, has a similar complaint about the town of Castelnuovo: 'the modern and unpicturesque successor to the former city'. The ancient Castelnuovo was entirely destroyed in the great earthquake of February 1783, described by Kappel Craven in his *Tour through Naples:*

'On the 5th February, 1783, a day indelibly stamped upon the recollection of every older native of this plain, all the towns and villages situated within this circuit were overthrown by the terrific shock, which extended far into Upper Calabria on one side, and reached Sicily on the other . . . At Castelnuovo every edifice was cast to the earth . . . At Terranova one straight street, containing 700 inhabitants, remains in the midst of ruins, which are those of a town of 13,000 souls . . . Three particular days, the 5th and 7th of February, and the 28th of March of the year 1783, are recorded as the periods of the most severe efforts of the convulsion; but six successive weeks from the first of these dates would perhaps be more correctly asigned to the continued internal fever, marked during that period by not less than a *thousand* distinct shocks; these were neither periodical nor attended by any particular symptoms in the state of the temperature. The summer of the preceding year had been remarkably hot, and followed by violent and continued rains till the month of January. The winter was rather more severe than usual, as may be inferred by the frost on the night of the 5th and 6th of February. It has been observed that this month and the following have in these regions been marked by the recurrence of four several earthquakes of more than ordinary violence.

'A thick fog succeeded the spring, and seemed suspended over all Calabria for some months, obscuring its shores from navigators, and only indicating their proximity by existence, so unusual in these latitudes. It is difficult to imagine a more extraordinary picture than the appearance of this portion of Italy, during the first few months which followed this awful visitation, by which an extent of territory exceeding 140 miles was more or less laid waste, and which can only be assimilated to the dissolution of the human energies and frame, under the activity of the operation of a violent poison. Here the finest works of nature, and the improvement they had received from the industry of man, were swept away by the same terrible agency which hurled mountains from their bases, and checked rivers in their speed. The convulsion extended from sea to sea, and the wreck throughout was universal. The wretched survivors fled from the few buildings which might have afforded shelter, while they only threatened destruction; and either wandered round the ruins which had overwhelmed the bodies of their friends and relations, or, mutilated and disabled, lay in hopeless apathy among their vineyards and fields, now affording neither fruit nor vegetation. These, as well as the necessaries of life, which the fertility of soil and benignity of climate render so abundant in these provinces, were involved in the general destruction; mills and magazines were annihilated; the wine and oil which could be saved had suffered such singular and offensive alterations as to render them useless; and even the water was not drinkable. All domestic animals seemed struck with an instinct of terror, which suspended their faculties; while even the wilder species were deprived of their native shyness and ferocity. The stillness of the air was remarkable, and contributed to render more appalling the deep-seated thunder which rumbled in the recesses of the earth, and every fresh throe was responded to by the apprehensive lamentations of the human, or the howls and screams of the brute creation.'

Dubrovnik and Lokrum

However much the experienced Yugoslav traveller insists that Dubrovnik is a tourist trap, a clip joint, not typical of the real Yugoslav spirit, pay no attention to him. Dubrovnik is a Venice without canals; a lovely walled city half surrounded by water, and moreover a city where you have the rare privilege of walking at ease, for no wheeled traffic is allowed inside the gates.

If you arrive by sea your ship will put in at the harbour of Gruz, and once on shore you will take a tram down to the old city. These trams are a delight, single-deckers, running on a very narrow-gauge rail and packed at all times of day. Here you may prefer to wander about alone but if you decide to take a guided tour, this is not as painful as it may sound, for your guide will speak excellent English, ensure that you see the Onofrio fountain, the Franciscan monastery with its superb cloister, the Rector's Palace, the attractive market. Then he may walk you up streets of steps, high above the squares and churches and on and up to the ancient walls, and there you have a view over the town and out to sea and across to the Zarcoviça Hill behind you. After this you will lunch at one of the large hotels—they're good—or in a converted convent which be-comes a night club after dark and where the young gather to dance late into the night.

On our last visit to Dubrovnik, after a long and excellent lunch at the Hotel Excelsior, presided over by our 75 year old host who knew Dubrovnik before, during and just after the last war, we were persuaded by him to make an excursion to the island of Lokrum, which we could see from the terrace of the hotel. There were no large organised parties down at the jetty waiting to embark, and we made a deal with an old, withered man to take the five of us over to the island in his rowing boat.

Fortified by a swig or two from a bottle of local wine the old man rowed us over to Lokrum and we disembarked at a rough jetty, arranging that he should meet us there in two hours time.

They tell you that Richard Cœur de Lion was shipwrecked off Lokrum in 1191 and was given hospitality by the monks; this monastery was destroyed in 1667 by a great earthquake but the ruins remain; beside and around them is a palace built by the Archduke Maximilian who bought the island in 1859. But he spent little time there since in 1864 he was cozened by Napoleon III into going to Mexico as Emperor; and there he was shot by Juarez in 1867. His wife, Carlotta, according to local legend, died of grief in this house, but that poor lady had many homes after her return to Europe on her mission to see the Pope and beg his intercession and aid for her husband. Part of the house, for Palace is a grandiose word, is a children's home and nearby there is a good small museum with collections of the flora and fauna of the Dubrovnik district.

The gardens were laid out for the Emperor with cypresses, cedars of Lebanon, pines, palms, a tiny maze like a knee high knot garden; and a belvedere. All this is beautifully maintained and the whole island is planted to give shady walks and many pretty vistas.

Some of our small party explored the garden; others played about in the rock pools and swam from the rocks; but we gathered together again and went down to the jetty. No boat-man. We explained in a mixture of shocking Serbo-Croat and Italian to one of the fishermen that we were looking for the owner of this boat. He laughed, shrugged, shouted to one of his friends who laughed even more. But within a few minutes our boatman arrived. Perhaps we thought he was a little drunk, but who were we to be censorious?

So we embarked. He took up the oars and we set off. After five minutes or so, he reached under the seat and produced his bottle of wine and offered it round, shipping his oars and beaming with good will. We all drank politely. He finished the bottle in one good gulp, threw it overboard and set himself to row. Meanwhile the clouds had gathered and there was a mean little wind and a few drops of rain and we were still far from 'Dubro', as he kept saying, pointing away into the distance.

Again he shipped oars, fumbled under the seat and produced a really formidable bottle of the same strong, rough white wine. Again we all drank; some of our company were not drinkers, but not wishing to give offence, they did their best. We toasted him in a variety of languages; one of us offered to help him row, an offer which was indignantly refused and the one prudent member of the party put on her plastic mac against the now heavy rain. After two more pauses, toasts and shouts of 'Dubro' we finally reached the Old Harbour and the familiar jetty of Dubrovnik. And we left our old man, beaming with pleasure at the extra money we gave him, partly out of relief, partly because we were in a rush to get under cover from the almost tropical rain. Some of us had drunk a lot of wine, some had had a trying journey, but all of us remember the simple delights of the island of Lokrum.

Travellers with a Purpose

Few men have travelled to such purpose as the plant collectors whose work has enriched the world's farms and embellished its gardens. Of the celebrated ones only the late F. Kingdon-Ward belongs to our time, for the greatest of these travellers were Victorians. In 1956 Kingdon-Ward was looking for gentians in Yunnan.

'From the day I first saw *Gentiana sino-ornata* growing above Atuutzu, in Yunnan, to the day in November 1956 when I saw the Cambridge-blue gentian on the summit of Mount Victoria in Burma, I have been bewitched by these incomparable rock plants . . . It is a wonderful experience to come suddenly on colonies of gentians in full bloom. When the colour of rhododendrons has gone from the hills, a grass slope bestrewn with large clumps of gentian is a sight to be for ever cherished and remembered.

'I shall never forget first seeing *G. sino-ornata* growing wild. It was on a steep mountainside of loose hungry-looking scree soil, with lots of stones and many scattered bushes, and I came on it unexpectedly. The ascent was steep and rather tiresome, as I kept slipping. But it was the first time I had tried this route and I thought it might be worth while to persevere. When at last I came to the first gentians, deep blue with that hint of violet that you get on a sunny morning in the South China Sea, I felt it had indeed been worthwhile; the form and colour made an indelible impression.'

One does not have to go to Yunnan to enjoy such experiences. I remember a meadow outside Nantua in Savoy, mahogany red with the flowers of *Fritillaria meleagris*. And the down behind a small inn in the mountains between Burgundy and Switzerland where the grass was blued by myriads of *Gentiana vernum* flowers. And a marshy wood in New England where, carefully avoiding poison ivy growing as thick as brambles in an English

hedge, we came on a great colony of that glorious orchid
Cypripedium reginae.

The magnificent Tree Paeonies—Moutans—were long
known to Europeans and Americans only as cultivated plants
obtained from China and Japan. Many believed that they had
long been extinct in the wild until that great traveller Reginald
Farrer at last discovered one in March 1914 on the Kansu-Tibet
border,

'After a very long stage we reached our haven at the Street of
Happy Sons—Fu-erh-Gai—a tiny place, as pretty as are all these
little valley-villages, and with a promise of nobler rugged ridges
rising behind, while in front, across the beck, rose a long high
hillside all copsed and wooded and blurred with promise,
illuminated here and there with the tender pink of Pyrus or
Dipelta. In the quiet evening we crossed the stream and
ascended the woodland by different paths. My own object was
a specially rosy tree of Pyrus, to which I at last attained toil-
somely through the jungle, delayed only by one other new
beauty, a wild-rose just beginning to break out in arching
sprays of golden-yellow blossom. A lady-slipper was peering up,
indeed, amid the brushwood, but it was as yet too undeveloped
to be made out; it had, though, several buds to the stem, and
thus differed from all those with which I came in contact later.
So I sat at last and rested, gazing down the steep loess tracks to
the little village at my feet, so comfortable and pleasant-looking
in its grove of poplars, till my eye was caught by certain white
objects farther along the hillside, that were clearly too big by far
to be flowers, yet must certainly be investigated if only to find
out what clots of white wool, or yet whiter paper, surely could
be doing in the wild coppice, perked up here and there above
the small-fry of little barberries and so forth. Probably they had
some religious meaning, I would see.

'Through the foaming shallows of the copse I plunged and
soon was holding my breath with growing excitement as I
neared my goal, and it became more and more certain that I was

setting eyes on *Paeonia Moutan* as a wild plant. The event itself justified enthusiasm, but all considerations of botanical geography vanish from one's mind in the first contemplation of that amazing flower, the most overpoweringly superb of hardy shrubs. Here in the brushwood it grew up tall and slender and straight, in two or three unbranching shoots, each one of which carried at the top, elegantly balancing, that single enormous blossom, waved and crimped into the boldest grace of line, of absolute pure white, with featherings of deepest maroon radiating at the base of the petals from the boss of golden fluff at the flower's heart. Above the sere and thorny scrub the snowy beauties poise and hover, and the breath of them went out upon the twilight as sweet as any rose.'

The Truth about Italian

The only writer who tells the whole truth about speaking Italian—that no foreigner ever does so correctly—Aubrey Menen in *Speaking the Language like a Native:* 'The principal weapon the Italian uses to keep the foreigner in his place is his quickness of mind. The second is the Italian language.

'The foreigner in Italy need not speak Italian. The people of the country pride themselves on their knowledge of foreign tongues, and they prefer to address a stranger in his own language. Everywhere in Italy there can be found someone who can speak some English, French or German. Not much, it is true: the Italian limits his vocabulary of foreign words. The foreigner will find that it is usually extensive enough to answer the needs of a not too exacting chimpanzee—food, water, shelter and elementary sexual satisfaction. Should the stranger aspire to talk of higher things, he will be in trouble. The Italian's vocabulary fades away until there is nothing left of him but his smile.

'So the foreigner sets himself to learn the language of the country he is in, and then he lands himself in even worse trouble . . .'

Why? Well, as Mr Menen explains, first there is the pronunciation: in every word made of vowels every vowel must be pronounced clearly and distinctly, for example in *aimoli*, flowerbeds. To form diphthongs of any two or more vowels makes you sound like an unlettered peasant. Worse, there is the grammar, the difficulty of which Mr Menen demonstrates as follows:

'. . . I have Maria in the summer-house. I now wish to say, "If only you knew how much I adore you"; I am not only in love, which is delightful, I am in the subjunctive mood, which is the very devil . . .'

There is still more, inflexion, and again I turn to Mr Menen for an example:

'A Neapolitan is sitting alone in his room. He owes the rent, he is broke, he has no job and no prospects. He has sold everything of value that he possesses and in this state is sitting hopelessly by the telephone wondering when the company is going to cut it off. The telephone rings, he picks it up. A bright and cheerful voice at the other end asks, "Is that the Bank of Naples?" to which he replies with one word—"*Magari*".'

Magari means, among several other things, 'scarcely' or 'hardly' in the ironical sense. Mr Menen tried it when a voice on his own phone asked if he was the Presidential Palace? '*Magari*.' Telephone: 'I asked you a civil question and expect a civil answer'—bang! Right word; wrong inflexion.

Roman Remains

The traveller who wants to see for himself how the imperial
Romans built cities can probably not do better than pay a visit
to Leptis Magna, seventy miles east of Tripoli. He will need a
car, of course, and the roads, shaded by the eucalyptus trees
which have been Australia's invaluable gift to all arid countries,
are quite good. The emperor Septimus Severus having been
born at Leptis, when he came to power embellished the city with
buildings in the most grandiloquent of the heavy Roman style,
using Italian, Greek and Asian marbles, and great monolithic
columns of granite shipped along the coast from Egypt. And he
enlarged and improved the artificial harbour. Leptis remained a
great city until it was sacked and half ruined by the Vandals.
For centuries, the Arabs being indifferent to the past, the
buildings were cannibalised for their dressed stone. But in 1911
the Italians occupied Libya; and thereafter their archaeologists
began to unearth and restore what their ancestors had built.

That Spanish Cow

'Il parle le français comme une vache espagnole . . .' But why
on earth a Spanish cow? Well, of course, it isn't. It's a corruption of '. . . 'Basque espagnol'—a people who usually can speak
French, but abominably. Not that most Frenchmen know it.

The Lenin Shrine

It is properly called the Lenin Museum, this extraordinary collection of Leniniana in Moscow and is in some ways the most remarkable spectacle in the city. Readers of George Orwell's *1984* will recall that Winston Smith's job was to re-write and cause to be reprinted back numbers of *The Times*, to make the past fit the Party's present policy, and history bear out the Party's wisdom. There is a very remarkable instance of this kind of truth-adjustment in the Lenin Museum. Among an amazing collection of relics—fire-irons, garments, reconstructions of Lenin's camp in Siberia etc.—of paintings in the 'heroic' style, books, bad sculpture, and of remarkable early family photographs, there is a large collection of newspaper and other public photographs covering as far as possible the whole of Lenin's life and above all his political activities. Among these are numerous group photographs, like those taken of football teams or wedding parties, of the Bolshevik leaders at various stages of the Revolution and first Bolshevik government. They have every appearance of being absolutely authentic; but in not one of them does Trotsky appear. Since he was, for years, by far the most important man in the Party and in the Government, after Lenin himself; and inseparable from Lenin in the leadership, the only explanation would seem to be that these photographs have been brilliantly faked to eliminate him. It could be that only photographs in which Trotsky did not, for some reason, appear, have been used. The faking hypothesis seems more likely, since there can hardly have been a large choice of photographs. Either way, the impression made on the groups of children and young people we saw being solemnly and reverently conducted round the exhibition must be the same— grossly misleading as to the facts.

The Party is, in short, in much the same difficulty as the Pope endowed with infallibility; forced to behave as if—to borrow from Orwell—while all its judgements are infallible and policies right, some are more infallible than others.

Incidentally only one photograph had Stalin in it—as a young man and very much in the background.

And the Tomb

For more than forty years an unbroken queue of the Faithful has been shuffling slowly through Lenin's tomb, in the Red Square, in the shadow of the Kremlin. Among these are old, wrinkled-faced *baboushkas*, bundled up in coats and shawls. Some of them utter a short prayer in front of the mummy; and perhaps, surreptitiously, cross themselves. It seemed to me that their very existence, poor old things, with all the classical stigmata of poverty short of starvation upon them, mocked the agonised spirit of the man-god they were worshipping. Outside, the whole vast expanse of the Red Square was empty, a space big enough for twenty polo games. The people were crowded, controlled by ropes and soldiers, round the periphery. It was May and the sun shone but the north-east wind was bitter and old people huddled from it, tourists from the Southern Republics turned blue, and the soldiers were stiff in their stout great-coats. In that immense cobbled *maidan* only one figure moved, apart from the queue, far away on the other side, shuffling into the Tomb: an old granny, bundled like all her kind in layers of subfusc, dirty clothes and a head shawl, who was sweeping the many acres of the square—with a sort of dustpan and brush. Poor old lady Hercules. If Lenin was, indeed, up there, among the just, as the muttered prayers of others of her kind before his pickled corpse implied, did he weep the dread tears of the dead for the vanity of living hopes, and the failure of a mission?

The Language of Women

Going up in the lift at our hotel in Moscow, the lift-woman, a
stout lady of perhaps fifty, but maybe only thirty, (it's hard to
tell there), who was studying geometry out of a school text-book,
wanted to know if Mary had children; and if so, how many.
When Mary failed to understand the question, she hit her, in a
hearty way peculiar to Muscovites, on the belly with the back of
her hand, and then held up four, three, two fingers. Mary held
up two and said, in halting Russian, 'two daughters'. The lift
woman had a colleague of similar burly figure in the lift with her.
They laid their big hands on Mary and kneaded. No corsets.
Their eyes marvelled at each other.

Misunderstandings in the USSR

A television programme in Moscow made much of London's
sale of London Bridge to the Americans. Several of our acquaintances commiserated with us on being thus reduced to the
expedient of selling our cultural heritage to the arch-imperialists.

Odessa; at the top of the grand Potemkin staircase. Our guide
and interpreter greets us with a long face. She had news for us
which, she regrets, must certainly distress us deeply. Mr
Robert Kennedy had been assassinated. As we had no acquaintance with Mr Kennedy our distress was as moderate as that of
any ordinary, sane man at the death of a merely public (to him)
person. It was difficult to live up to our guide's apparent expec-
tations: we sent for no ashes, no sackcloth. A politician had

fallen victim to an occupational hazard. How sad; on the same day a few score other Americans, a few hundred Vietnamese, had died by violence; how sad.

But Soviet citizens are, or at all events seem to be, different. Incredible though it may seem, we heard well authenticated stories of people who wept when Stalin died. Alexander Solzhenitsyn, perhaps the greatest living novelist, bears witness to this same astounding perversion of emotion. And we had yet another instance of it.

We are half way through our long, gruelling but fascinating tour of the Nikitsky Sad, the great botanic garden at Yalta, one of the half dozen most beautiful gardens in the world. The Assistant Director, our guide in the absence of his chief, choosing a belvedere with a glorious view over the lower arboretum and the sapphire of the Black Sea, suddenly makes his face very grave—until then we had been all smiles—and says something to his colleague, a stout and jolly biologist, who, having a good command of English, was our interpreter. She turns to us and says, gravely, 'Ah, yes, we are sorry but we have very, very bad news for you.'

Mary has visions of Victoria having been run over by a bus on the way to school. I wonder if de Gaulle has finally declared war on Harold Wilson. The biologist having thus braced us, says, 'Mr Randolph Churchill has died.'

I don't know how many people die every minute. We were as moved by Mr Randolph Churchill's death as Mr Randolph Churchill would have been by ours. It was a disappointment to our Soviet hosts. There is no doubt about it, they expected us to mourn the death of a man we had never met.

Taxi Drivers

Cab drivers in Rio de Janeiro have, it seems, always been notorious for mad driving. In *Across Patagonia*, a remarkable late 19th century account of an exploring, guanaco-hunting and 'ostrich'-hunting expedition, by Lady Florence Dixie, the authoress describes a hair-raising cab drive down to the docks in Rio, which ended in the wildly galloping mules taking a corner too fast and turning the vehicle over, hurling Lady Florence, her husband and her two brothers, Lord Queensberry and Lord John Douglas, into the road. They suffered no injuries which, as Lady Florence says in her brisk and jolly way, could not be cured by a bit of court plaster when they got back on board their ship. The heirs of that mule-driving cabby are today's Rio taxi-drivers; they all drive Volkswagens and they race like lunatics, but at least they are cheerful, know their city inside out, and are polite.

New York taxi-drivers are of two kinds: the savagely surly, and the intolerably talkative. The latter don't just talk to you, they lecture you, shouting over one shoulder as they drive; even worse are those who expect answers, for you have to join in the shouting match. One realises how blessed we Londoners are in the design of our taxis and one prays that the police will never allow it to be changed, or ordinary saloon cars to be used. As for the surly drivers, they look at you with the contempt you deserve for thinking you can get about New York in a taxi, shrug when you name your destination as if you must be out of your mind, or simply malicious, in asking him to drive you to such a place; and answer any remark on the density of the traffic jam with a snarl.

In Melbourne, in Sydney and in Christchurch, New Zealand, taxi-drivers are civil, helpful, quiet-spoken men who seem content with their lot. The same is true in San Francisco. Maybe they're better paid in those places; or perhaps it's a matter of climate. In Singapore they are Chinese, cheerful, even laughing, and drive like fiends. In Calcutta they are Sikhs and bad tempered, but it's a bad-tempered place and their vehicles are such jalopies as would try any driver's temper.

Thirty, forty years ago Paris taxi-drivers were a high-spirited, dashing body of men, cutting the corners by charging over the sidewalk, treating the police with laughing contempt, and getting you from A to B quicker than any other drivers in the world. Now, broken by sitting helpless in interminable traffic jams, at least on the *rive gauche*, poisoned by exhaust fumes and discouraged by poverty, they are a sad, *piano* race, civil if spoken to but deeply depressed.

Public Transport in the USSR

In many towns of the USSR much of the public transport is run on a more intelligent system than ours—as an essential public service, and not as an undertaking intended to make a profit. On many, perhaps most, but for some reason not all buses and trolley-buses, there is no conductor. Fixed in two or three places in the vehicle are rolls of tickets and a slotted box for the money. The money box is not an automatic device releasing the tickets; it is a simple metal box. You just take your ticket and drop in your money. In short, there is a trust system. We asked whether there were not people who took advantage of it to ride free; Yes; but the lowest paid workers were not intended to pay; and as for the others, there were not many. This we were able to verify for ourselves; on a very crowded bus from the outskirts to the centre of Odessa, a journey taking nearly half-an-hour, we were standing nearest to one of the rolls of tickets and spent the whole journey putting money, passed from hand to hand, in the box for the other passengers, and passing tickets back. Whether there is or is not a conductor—when there is it is always an elderly woman who remains seated and expects passengers to bring her their fares—there is only one fare whatever the journey-length—4 kopeks. Even at the falsely low value of the £ sterling fixed by the inequitable exchange rate for the rouble, this is under 5 old or 2 new pence.

We think of the Soviet citizen as cowed by authority. He, and above all she, is certainly not 'disciplined' when it comes to public transport. The scramble for buses or trolley-cars in Moscow is as disorderly as in Paris. We saw some spectacular rows in taxi queues; and if a policeman did step across to see what the uproar was about, he usually withdrew with a shrug, especially if a couple of formidable Muscovite matrons laden with shopping were involved. On one occasion, however, a Moscow policeman did intervene to see that we, diffident aliens, a dozen times jostled or tricked out of our turn, got a cab. They are, by the way, cheap and very fast.

Even boarding aeroplanes for internal flights is such a free-for-all that Intourist guides always arrange to get foreigners seated before the natives are unleashed, to be more or less controlled by stewardesses who seem to have been chosen, and wisely, rather for their muscularity and sturdy, powerful frames, than for charm.

Meals on Aeroflot internal flights are not for gourmets but one has to remember that flying is much cheaper in the USSR than anywhere outside it.

Gomera by Sea

Of the seven Canary Islands two cannot be reached by air; la Gomera and el Hierro. For the travellers seeking the less trodden places, la Gomera has much to offer. It is reached by sea from Santa Cruz de Tenerife or from Las Palmas de Gran Canaria; and as a rule the passage is an overnight one. In the calm, mild climate of the archipelago those few hours at sea are very pleasant, although the ships are not luxurious and the first class, two-berth cabins are very small.

The port and capital of the island is San Sebastian de la Gomera. It is a quiet and undistinguished little town. There are no hotels, but two or three *pensiones* which are clean, comfortable and very cheap. And there are only two buildings of interest; the Torre del Conde built, about 1450, by Hernan Peraza, lord of Gomera and, in theory, of some of the other islands by right of purchase; and the parish church of San Sebastian, the last place where Christopher Columbus prayed before the last and longest leg of that voyage which ended in the discovery of America.

Columbus had an earlier connection with the island. As agent for a Genoese firm of merchants, in Madeira, he had done business with the Canary Islands. At the court of Isabella the Catholic he had met Beatriz de Bobadilla, whose celebrated beauty had seduced Ferdinand of Aragon and caused the queen to get rid of her by confining her to La Gomera, her fief. There is a legend of a passionate love affair between Columbus and Beatriz; but the only evidence is of business dealings between them, for on his second voyage to America, in 1493, it was in San Sebastian that Columbus bought the farm and domestic animals, and seeds of crops which he wanted to introduce into America.

La Gomera is an island of quite extraordinary beauty; in form it is simply a hemisphere of rugged mountains divided into wedge-shaped 'slices' by deep ravines called *barrancos*.

This makes travel by land extremely difficult; there is only one good motor road, and one other road just possible in the best conditions, for a jeep, or even a motor car driven slowly and carefully; for the rest, you must either walk or ride a mule. The Gomerans use a small coasting steamer to get their goods and themselves round the island.

The good road runs through and over mountains and indescribably magnificent scenery, through the small towns and fertile, richly planted valleys of Hermigua and Agulo, to Tamargada almost on the sea, inland again to the glorious Vallehermoso, and finally back to the seashore at Puerto de Vallehermoso. In the centre of the island is primaeval forest country, the Montes del Cedro, mostly the big evergreen laurel, *Laurus canariensis* and the great, white-flowered and very fragrant tree-heather, *Erica arborea* often reaching thirty or forty feet in height and with trunks two or three feet in girth. The island crops include dates, citrus, bananas, paw-paws and, of course, wine.

But the most remarkable distinction of La Gomera is the whistled language called *Silbo*. It is not a code of whistles, but whistled Spanish in which variations in pitch and tone of whistling replace the modulated vibration of vocal chords. Communication by *Silbo* is possible over several miles—the range is enormously greater than that of the ordinary voice and there is much less loss of clarity over great distances than in shouting.

The Spaniards learnt *Silbo* from the native Guanches. In the course of the battle, in Tenerife, which ended in the Spaniards' devastating defeat by this Stone Age people without metal weapons, the Guanche captains, by using *Silbo* to communicate orders to the several detachments of their army, were able to manœuvre it without giving away their intention to the enemy, a fact which had much to do with their victory.

Curiously enough, *Silbo* would not be possible in any other European language; Professor André Classe of Glasgow

University, the greatest academic authority on the subject, has pointed out that it is the relatively simple articulation of Spanish which makes it possible to whistle it. Had the conquerors of the Canary Islands been French or English, it seems probable that *Silbo* would not have survived.

Kiev

If I had to live in the USSR I should choose Kiev to settle in. It is one of the pleasantest and most beautiful, most amusingly busy and yet relaxed cities I have seen anywhere in the world, with all the confidence and graces of a capital. Magnificently sited on and towering heights above the Dnieper, so great is the river and so busy its traffic of freighters, passenger ships, pleasure streamers and lighters, yachts, racing eights and water skiers, that the city has all the liveliness of a major port and holiday centre as well as fascinating views of the river and its life. Surrounded by wooded hills, the city itself is very handsome, with wide boulevards shaded on each side by avenues of fine trees bordering broad walks, and handsome bridges over the river. Shops and restaurants are better than elsewhere in the USSR with the possible exception of Leningrad. The people have the easy temper, good manners and sense of humour proper to the citizens of an ancient capital; civilization, flourishing commerce, arts, letters and music are all much older in Kiev than in Moscow. Theatres and cinemas and well-served concert halls are numerous. Kiev has 150 parks, some tiny, no more than squares of grass, with a few trees, others very large. In all quarters it is a city of fine trees. Its botanic gardens, among the best in the world, sited on top of a hill above the city, are particularly good for their wild sections, each planted after

nature with the flora of one part of the Union. The gardens
slope down towards the river in many places, and there are
lovely glimpses of the water, shipping, and beyond them, of
golden domed churches.

Saint Sophia's Cathedral is sublime; begun in 1037, at about
the same time as Canterbury Cathedral, its golden domes were
added later. It shines in the sunshine like an immense jewel.
The church has a fine collection of ancient ikons and murals.

The new residential quarter, sited very high and composed
of tall blocks of flats, is well-designed and built, with more style
and colour than one sees in other Soviet cities. Trailing plants
were being trained from balcony to balcony and there were
many well-planted window boxes. The city is full of schools—
it is the seat of an ancient university and of many modern
technical colleges; and that, again, gives it a lively population
of young men and women.

Nor are these things all; you can take ship at Kiev and spend
three days in a fascinating cruise by way of Cherkassy,
Kremencing, Dniepropetrosk (the ancient Ekaterinoslav),
Nikospal and Kherson and thence into the Black Sea, crossing
the mouth of the Bug, to Odessa. How far up the river you can
go by steamer or launch, or up the Desna which meets the
Dnieper at Kiev, I did not enquire. But from Odessa you can
tranship to Yalta, Chekov's lovely hilly little town on the Black
Sea, on the South-east of the Crimean Peninsula.

Passports and Money

Passports have been so much a part of foreign travel since 1920
that there are hundreds of thousands of people, even experienced travellers, who do not realise that we, in the 'seventies,

do not know what freedom in travelling means. Before 1914 most travellers never had or so much as saw a passport and any Englishman or American was free to get on a ship and go anywhere in the world. Only in the Russian Empire was he apt to be bothered by the police. He could apply for a passport if he knew that he was going to Russia or to some other country where travelling was, or might be, restricted but there was no police control in West Europe or America.

Pre-1914, the travelling citizen was freer than we are in another respect: it had not occurred to any government to impose upon its citizens rules about how much of their own money they could spend where. And since all currencies were in gold coin there was virtually a universal currency.

In a travel guide book to Europe published for Americans in 1900, the reader is advised about passports: 'Shall we take a passport on our tour? On the whole, yes. You will not be asked to show it in any of the countries included in this book, but it may be useful as a means of identification at banking-houses and it will occasionally serve as an *open sesame* to public buildings, art galleries and the like, if you seek admission at other than the regular hours or without the required ticket of admission.'

It is customary for passport inspection officers to ask to see your passport as you pass through the sea or airport on your way out of the country and a majority of modern British travellers undoubtedly think of this as a part of the necessary formalities; they are under the impression that they cannot get out of the country without showing their passport. In fact, however, the Home Office have no right to ask to see your passport as you leave the country; nobody has. And you can refuse to show it.

If you do so it will be explained to you that inspection is for your own protection; if your passport is not in order you may be refused entry to the country you're going to.

I once took a hasty decision to go to Paris for a few days on business. At London Airport a passport inspector horrified me by saying, politely: 'Mr Hyams, your passport expired last month. It is not valid.' I had known, but had forgotten, that it was about due for renewal. This did not mean that I could not go to Paris; I had to sign a chit for the airline exonerating them from responsibility, so that I could not claim my fare back if the French refused me entry; for the rest it was up to me, I could go, and take a chance with the French passport control. I had a bad quarter of an hour just before passport control at Orly airport. But either the French did not notice the date on my passport, or did not care that it was out of date. Nothing was said.

I have never found that running out of money abroad is a serious disaster. In a surprisingly large number of foreign countries people have until very recently, been willing to take an Englishman's personal cheque, especially where there are Indian shop-keepers. But I have had some disconcerting money adventures abroad. Leaving Spain, in my very ancient car, a month or so after the Civil War broke out in 1936, the only money I had, apart from £3 sterling, was in pesetas. No French bank would buy them, and I had to get to Calais on that £3. It was worth about £10 of our present money. In Albany, New York, in 1938, a major bank refused to cash a travellers' cheque issued by the Midland Bank Limited: they'd never heard of it.

On the other hand: in 1940 I was in Arles and had just paid my hotel bill when the news of the German break-through and of the chaos in the north, reached us. The hotelier, who did not know me, came and asked me how much money I had left. I said I had my train ticket and enough pocket-money to get me to Calais or Boulogne. He insisted on knowing the actual sum, so I told him. He pointed out that the journey might be prolonged and difficult—it was—; and he not only insisted on my taking back the money I had just paid him, but provided a big hamper of food, in case of emergencies. When as soon as possible after the war, I called to repay him, he at first refused to accept money from '*un de nos libérateurs*'. Perhaps I need hardly say that it was his wife who told him not to be such a fool, and who took the money from my hand, and counted it.

Steam Coaches

There is a popular, complacent notion that 'you can't stop progress'. But a means of transport which would have represented great progress in its time was stopped very successfully by the mail coach and horse-coping interests, though it did them no good for shortly afterwards began the great age of railways.

Between 1820 and 1840 a number of transport engineers were experimenting with steam-driven coaches which were to use the same roads as the horse-drawn coaches. The vehicles built and tried would, when their teething troubles were overcome (which they soon would have been for there was nothing seriously wrong with them), have been faster than horse-drawn coaches, would have carried more passengers, had a greater payload and above all been much cheaper than horse-drawn coaches. The average speed aimed at was 15 m.p.h. and the projects were backed by substantial capitalists.

What chiefly worried the horsey interests was the threat of much cheaper transport. It is not generally realised that travel, before the age of mechanical transport, was exorbitantly dear. Mail coach fares for passengers were 6d. a mile outside, 1/- a mile inside, at a time when the labourer's wage in England was 5/- a week. A journey of 100 miles inside a mail coach cost the passenger £5—a sum which one could live on very comfortably for a month, including one's rent. Air transport in 1970 is about 1/- a mile; that shilling is not worth one tenth of the mail coach passenger's shilling. The mail coach interests had, in short, a 'licence to coin money' and were prepared to use every possible means to defend it.

The method which answered their purpose was that of lobbying and bribing M.P.s when Turnpike Franchise Bills came before the House of Commons for renewal, so that prohibitively high road tolls were imposed on mechanically propelled vehicles using the turnpike roads—the only good ones available to them. These tolls were fixed so high that the advantages of steam traction were wiped out and steam coaches were unable to compete with horse-drawn vehicles.

It could not happen now? How do you know?

Travel in 1900

From a guide-book to European travel for Americans:
'If you are going abroad for a season of travel take almost nothing. It is as well to start with but one dress beside the one you use on the steamer—anything you chance to have: a black alpaca, or half-worn black silk is very serviceable. When you reach Paris, circumstances, and the season will govern your purchases; and this same dress will be almost a necessity for constant railway journeys, rainy day sightseeing and mule-riding in Switzerland . . .'

'For an educated American youth to have no knowledge of architecture . . . he would not be fitted to visit Westminster Abbey. Let him defer his voyage a year, until he knows the difference between a spire and a tower, a groin or a gable.'

'In Great Britain the average cost of living at a good second-class hotel need not exceed eight or nine shillings a day exclusive of liquors; and by dining at eating-houses it may be reduced to seven shillings, or even less. In France the franc will go as far as the shilling does in Great Britain.'

'English sovereigns are current money in all the countries through which our route lies; but French 20 franc pieces or *Napoleons* as they continue to be called, are better on the Continent.' (the route included Belgium, France, Switzerland and Italy).

'On landing in Europe we have to go through the customs house . . . It should be borne in mind that even a single copy of an American reprint of an English copyrighted book is liable to be confiscated.' (Until 1920 American publishers swindled British authors by pirating their books, paying no royalty.)

'For a (European) tour of four months, all necessary expenses (allowing $125 for a return ocean passage) may be covered by $400. This could be reduced somewhat by one who has a knowledge of French and German. (In English currency, £80 at the current rate of exchange—i.e. £20 a month) . . . It requires that, forethought and prudence is not necessarily an overanxious counting of the pennies, nor any self-denial inconsistent with good living, good health and hearty enjoyment.' (Elsewhere this author says that it is the English part of the tour which is dear. On the Continent one can do very well on an expenditure of 5/- a day.)

Motels in the USA

If the *caravanserai* is the oldest kind of rest-house for travellers, the motel is the newest and it is at its best in America where it was invented. I have stayed in motels in half-a-dozen states: the rooms are larger than in American hotels, equally well-equipped with heating, cooling, television etc., as well or better furnished; and much cheaper.

One we stayed at in the Blue Mountains of Virginia was quite excellent. It had only one flaw; when we came in after a morning's exploring on horseback, and went to what was called the Tap Room, we discovered for the first time that Virginia is a semi-dry state, spirits being forbidden. Mary, reading the drinks card, found however, that both Guinness and New York 'champagne' were to be had. So we decided to drink Black Velvet. As the barman had never heard of it, we asked for a bottle of the 'champagne', a pint bottle of Guinness and a large glass jug; and, under the fascinated eyes of the whole room, concocted the mixture for ourselves. It is certainly the best way of making use of New York champagne.

It was on riding expeditions from that motel that I discovered that where there is an interesting shrubby flora, botanising on horseback is better than botanising on foot, provided you you have a quiet horse; and our hacks could not have been quieter. Being mounted brings you on a level with the flowers.

We liked best of all the very small, country motels in New England, with ten or twelve cabins and a simple dining-room, run by a man and his wife, with some casual help. The cabins, usually pleasantly screened by trees, are well furnished with two beds, shower, heating and cooling and the ubiquitous television. The food, mostly grills, is good, especially the egg and bacon breakfasts. And they cost about the same as an English country-town hotel, which is to say that they are, for America, remarkably cheap. The people are usually pleasant

and friendly. If you want drinks—wine or beer or spirits—
you must bring your own.

The least comfortable motel we stayed in was near Miami,
but that was because we had no car there—I had mislaid my
driving licence and could not hire one; and because we were
caught in the skirts of a hurricane and walking was either
impossible or very disagreeable. Exceptionally, the place had
no dining-room and we had to walk an uncomfortable mile for
every meal. Some American towns—Miami and Los Angeles
for two—are not built for people but for motorcars, with no
footpaths outside the city centre, and the whole place sprawling
over a vast territory so that wherever you want to go to is a long
way from where you are.

Bar Customs

Motoring through the lovely country and exquisite neo-classical
style small towns of New England is delightful but has strange,
archaic hazards. About noon, coming to a larger, more truly
urban town—the old New England towns are really garden-
towns and often seem to have no centre—we decided to stop
for a drink. We parked the car and went into a respectable
looking saloon and took our seats on stools at the bar. In
addition to the barman, an etiolated creature with spots and no
chin, there were half-a-dozen men in the place. They all turned
and stared, coldly outraged. The barman hurried along to us:
'That young lady cain't set there.'

'Why not?'

'No ladies at the bar. She wants a drink she better set at that
table.'

Even though she did sit at the table, the spectacle of her drinking whisky seemed to cause them pain. Drinking, like dirty talk, (hence the bar rule, general in all the New England states we visited), is for men.

In Melbourne, Australia, the temperature being in the eighties, I was wearing light grey mohair trousers, a Chinese silk shirt and an Italian silk tie. We went into one of the bars of a large hotel. I was immediately asked to leave. Having no jacket, I was unsuitably dressed for that bar; but could be served in another to which the scruffier types were banished. Same thing in Cape Town: Silk-shirted and tied, but jacketless, we had to have our drinks brought to us in a sort of lounge by an apologetic but adamant coloured waiter.

In Madrid we sat drinking in one of the smartest bars in the window seat. Outside in the street was a very battered-looking and rather dirty beggar, importuning passers-by. Presently, deciding he had done enough work for the morning, he entered the bar, sat down, and was served like any other man.

In Madras, armed with one Alcoholic's Card, we were directed to the Permit Room. We ordered two whiskies. The barman asked for two cards. I produced one, which upset the barman. But why—couldn't he simply mark two drinks off my card? No: 'treating' was not allowed. I could, of course, have two drinks—twenty, for that matter—myself. Very well: this lady would drink one of them for me, while he looked the other way. All right? He grinned. And that, thereafter, was how we drank in the Permit Room.

Rio: we drift by accident into the kind of place we avoid—an excessively smart, dark red, hideously expensive bar. At the bar two richly dressed and very drunk, elderly Americans. One, maudlin, was drooling on and on about the failure of some official mission which had brought him to Rio. The other, his face grey and green, his eyes glazed, repeated over and over again, the same consolation formula. Both were drinking treble gins as fast as the barman could pour them. To the occasional all-pals-together advance made by the maudlin drunk, he replied with curt contempt. He served their drinks with the expression of an orthodox Jew forced to pour swill for pigs. He served our drinks with a small smile and a little shrug of apology. They cost four times the price anywhere else in the city.

In a tiny bodega in a small village on the island of Fuerteventura. We order our drinks. The noisiest and largest man at a table of card-playing drinkers looks at the three of us, asks are we Germans, we confess to being only English. He shouts at the barman that our drinks are on him. I open my mouth to protest politely, but the barman gives me a quick, small but emphatic shake of the head. We are not allowed to pay for our drinks.

Two friends of mine were dining at a hotel in Leningrad. At the next table was a party of young Russians celebrating something. They called the waitress and gave her an order and presently a bottle of Ukrainian 'champagne' was brought to my friends' table, with their neighbours' compliments.

Soviet Communist Manners

Of the six heads of institutions whom we had to work with in the USSR, three, on introduction, bowed and kissed Mary's hand. It was the biggest surprise the country gave us.

Night Walkers

It is our practice and pleasure to walk strange cities at night. It is most rewarding in Italy and in France. In Rome you can make the Piazza Navona a goal, and sit on a café terrace drinking, watching the fantastic baroque fountains, and the 'Red Indian' flame and sword swallower whose haunt it is, and the people, until one in the morning. A possible goal, if you need one, in Paris is the Shakespeare Bookshop on the Quai des Orfèvres which stays open—or used to—into the small hours. In Rio, wandering late at night, we stumbled on a book market, too, stalls of books in every language filling a square shaded by tall palms.

In Madras we walked at night; but not in Calcutta, the city of dreadful night. No European not prepared to give up life as the West understands it, to sell all he has and give to the poor, to become such another as Loyola's disciple, Francis Xavier, can afford to get as near to the reality of human life for the majority of mankind as a nocturnal walk through Calcutta must bring him. A night drive, conducted by a man who knows the city, is enough.

In New York, too, we gave up the pleasure of night-walking. It should be understood that the same is not true of the other American cities; to wander about San Francisco or St. Louis at night is delightful. Although we were aware of the immanent violence of New York at night, a violence which too often becomes real, we did not at first take quite seriously our friends' refusal to let us walk home after a dinner party, or their warnings not to go walking the streets for an airing in the small hours before bed. One night we left the apartment which had been lent to us in East 76th street, walked through to Second Avenue, downtown a couple of blocks; we became aware that we were being followed, and loitered to get a look at the man. He had a dead white face, seemed to keep his eyelids so lowered that he could only see our feet, and with his hands in the pockets of an old, long overcoat, walked hunched. When we stopped to look into a shop window, so did he; when we walked on, so did he. We turned across town and walked towards Fifth Avenue, He still followed, very slowly shortening the distance between us.

We came to a drugstore with a coffee bar still open. We went in for coffee, hoping our follower would lose heart. He did not. When we came out he was still there. There seemed to be nobody but ourselves in the streets. He began to follow us again. By the time we had turned into 76th street we were hurrying.

Why? We were not in Central Park where feral men lurk to mug the imprudent burgess who dares to enter that reserve for those who have gone back to savagery. The proper course was to turn towards the man, go to him, ask him what he wanted. The fact is that the *mythus* of New York is demoralising, destructive of all charity. As much as Calcutta, this city, which we enjoy, needs a Francis Xavier. We know what would, surely, have happened had we had the humanity to turn towards our follower and speak to him. He would have backed away from us.

Beggars

One is sometimes begged off in London, usually by respectable looking elderly women, sometimes by loitering men whom you come to recognize. It goes without saying that you are pestered by beggars in India and other eastern cities and in all Arab countries. It is a question of desperate poverty but also of tradition whereby it is not shameful to ask and is meritorious to give. I have been begged off in all the European capitals; but never frightened by beggars, as we were in the New York

Bowery. We went for a walk there one Sunday morning but were virtually driven out of the neighbourhood by the aggressiveness of the beggars. They are all men, all drunks or 'wineos' and when they see you coming they make for you with a determination—or desperation—equal to any Arab's, and stay with you almost as persistently. But they do not touch your heart like the pitiable beggars, especially the women and children of, for example, Djakarta or Calcutta, or Southern Italy.

In Spain and Portugal begging has a kind of dignity, as if it were a recognized and by no means disreputable profession. I have never made up my mind whether this is a vestigial custom of mediaeval Christianity, which lingers in those very Catholic countries with such other ancient practices as persecution of Protestants; or whether it is a faint echo of Moorish manners. The first time I went to Spain, in the early 'thirties, I was warned not to refuse a beggar curtly or to ignore him. If I did not want to give alms, I should say, 'Forgive me, brother, for the love of God'; the beggar would then leave me in peace. But that was in Andalusia.

We visited a bird sanctuary centred on an islanded lake not far from Madras. Wherever we went we were followed by a whole tribe of small, pretty and well-fed Tamil children, including a baby carried in the arms of a six-year old Tamil girl. Their method of begging was to trot just at our sides, holding out their hands and persistently whispering 'Sahib, sahib . . .' We gave them every small coin we had in our pockets and handbags, but they still persisted, ruthless, expressionless, unmoved even by a pantomime of anger. An Indian friend told us, later: 'You should have turned on them and crossed your eyes. They would have run away.' Is this true? I don't know.

We were never begged for money anywhere in the USSR, not even in the Far East, but one day in a subway crossing a Moscow street some small boys came running up to us and said, in English, 'Will you give us a biro, please?' We looked blank: 'Veuillez nous donner un biro, s'il vous plaît?' When we still looked blank they tried us in German. We gave in and handed over our biros. They darted away like lightning without a word of thanks. It was not bad manners: they were afraid of some grownup interfering and chastising them for un-Soviet shamelessness.

We were walking one day along the *rive gauche* Quais in Paris when a well-dressed and personable young man came up to me and said, in English but with a French accent, 'Will you please give me one franc.'

'Certainly', I said.

And did so.

After all, why not?

More Kittens

There was one beautiful palm-lined avenue in Rio de Janeiro that Mary could not bear to walk down again. Returning to the hotel on the waterfront for lunch we saw a grey kitten inside some railings which enclosed a garden, breast high to the street. It was miserably thin and we saw that someone had left a few scraps of food for it on a paper. Mary can never pass a cat without wanting to talk to it, but as she did so she turned to me, horror struck. Near to the little animal was a burst-open brown paper parcel out of which protruded the head of another grey kitten, very dead. We left, she felt sick and helpless, but there is nothing that we could have done: we were leaving by aeroplane in a matter of days, and what was one kitten in a town where many starve up on the slopes of the mountains?

A day or so later, taking an evening walk with the rest of the inhabitants, we saw a small negro boy, sitting on a door-step crying bitterly. One or two motherly women called out to him as they passed by; he paid no attention, just screwed his fists tighter into his streaming eyes. We stopped and spoke to him; he could not understand our Portuguese, or Spanish, or English, but he recognised a tone of voice and looked at us, tears falling thick and fast. Mary held him close to her for a moment, I gave him some small coins which he clutched to his chest. Beside and around us the unheeding strollers continued their way, some laughing at our, and his predicament. We were as helpless with him as we were with the starving kitten, and for the same reason—our ways lay as ineluctably apart as parallel lines.

Ryoan-ji

Travellers who are not interested in gardens as we know them, gardens of plants and flowers, and who readily leave them out of their list of sights to be seen, should make an exception to that rule in Japan, and see at least one Dry Landscape garden, preferably the Ryoan-ji. From the 7th century until the mid-19th century garden-making, being an important religious act, was, in Japan, what it never was anywhere else in the world, one of the fine arts. Consequently the most celebrated gardens were never altered from time to time, never redesigned and differently planted, any more than our own great paintings were ever repainted. Those Japanese gardens which contain trees and shrubs have, of course, much in common with our own, superficially at least. But the Zen Buddhist gardens, product of a school of abstract artists using symbols older than Buddhism in Japan and working under the influence of Southern Sung monochrome landscape painting, are unique and altogether remarkable.

Ryoan-ji

It is probably true that the beauty, sense and feeling communicated by these gardens to Japanese educated in their own ancient culture are not wholly accessible to Europeans who may have conscientiously read what, just by way of a single example, the word *Horai* describes, and what the thing *Horai* means, but will certainly not feel, upon seeing a certain group of rocks, the significance of that symbol. But we can vouch for the fact that something of the remarkable power of these strange works of art is conveyed even to Europeans ignorant of the symbols and the significance of their arrangement.

The Ryoan-ji is a level oblong of coarse sand enclosed on three sides by a wall coped with a broad tiled roof and on the fourth by a very simple pavilion of painted timber, similarly roofed. In it are placed five groups each composed of two or three rocks of different sizes and shapes. The sand is raked in straight lines parallel with the long axis of the work; and in concentric circles round each group of rocks. The art of the Ryoan-ji lies in the use of the ancient meaning of each group of rocks, or rather meanings, for there has been a syncretism of elements drawn from several epochs in Japanese religious history; and in the aesthetic of the relative distances and directions of the groups of rock to each other and to the space as a whole. There are possible analogues with calligraphy and with typographical layout.

The point, however, is the remarkable effect of this apparently simple, immensely subtle work of art on the beholder. Sit down and look at it—only a few people are allowed in at one time—and the mind and heart become still and very quiet; for a few minutes serenity is attained.

Phrase

Phrase book jokes have become a bore. We are all only too well-acquainted with that eternal postilion who was struck by lightning. But our friend Mrs Eileen Hardie did give a new one worth recording, from an old Serbo-Croat phrase book in her collection.

At the Physician's.

Visitor: Doctor, I fear I have the pox.

Doctor: Very likely.

Discovery of the British Isles

'In a four months voyage, keeping to his left the great shoreless ocean on which no ship had ever ventured, where the breeze blows not, but eternal fogs rest upon its lifeless waters, Himilco reached the Aestrymnides. Rich are they in metals, tin and lead; spirited and industrious the race which inhabits them; fond, too, are they of trade, and traverse the boisterous sea not in ships of pine or oak, but in coracles made of skins sewn together. At a distance of two days sail from there is the Holy Isle with its abundance of green pastures, inhabited by the Hibernians; hard by lies the wide isle of Albion.'

The Victorian translation is of a fragment of metrical Latin paraphrase—the *Ora Maritima* of Festus Avienus, of a report made by their Admiral Himilco to the Senate of Carthage some time in the 5th century B.C. Himilco sailed north up the west coast of Europe looking for new sources of raw materials for Carthaginian industry, or of gold; and for new materials for

Carthaginian commerce. Note the forbidding description of the Atlantic, paralleled by Sataspe's account of the Atlantic off the west coast of Africa, as recorded in Herodotus (iv.43). The Carthaginian seamen were not, themselves, afraid of the ocean, but they had every intention of making sure that Greek maritime commerce stayed inside the Mediterranean.

The Leaning Tower

In all the arts there is a comic as well as a serious mood. So why not in architecture? It has long seemed to me that the Duomo in Milan is a good example of the comic mood in Gothic architecture; and the first time I set eyes on the leaning tower in Pisa, I laughed; and have laughed as at a familiar and beloved joke, each time I have seen it since.

The architect Bonnano began to build this marble campanile, part of the Duomo complex, in 1174. When it had reached a height of 30 feet, the ground under the foundations gave way and the campanile leaned sideways. Bonnano tried to get it vertical again, but failed. Then in 1235, despite the tilt, another architect, Gualielmo of Innsbruck, added three more floors, making seven in all. Over a century later Tomasso Pisano added an eighth floor for the belfry. This made the tower 179 feet high and 14 feet out of the vertical; but of late it has been tending to lean more acutely, and steps had to be taken to make it safe.

Going up the campanile by the spiral staircase between the double walls is disagreeable. Not only is there a feeling that the whole thing will fall over at any moment, but each time you reach the overhanging side there is a terrific pull which seems to be preventing you from climbing the stairs. But the view of the Duomo, and the town, and miles of flat, fertile country, is magnificent.

A curious effect of the singularity of this Leaning Tower has been that of obscuring the quality of the Duomo itself. Built between 1175 and 1663, the chief architect being Burchetto, it has one of the most beautiful façades in Italy. The acoustics of the building are peculiar: sing four notes in succession, and the echo returns them as a chord.

Parthenon Ruins

The Parthenon we admire with such fervour is a ruin. I have wondered whether we should find so much to love in it, were it still as its builders made it. Gaunt, austere and graceful on its acropolis, violence and time have given it that lightness, airiness, which we admire in our own most beautiful temples—a minimum of lines and masses defining a maximum of space. Violence has done more than time to change it; the temple was used by the Turks as an ammunition store; hit by a shell, the ammunition exploded; it is a wonder so much of the building still stands. When, a solid block against the sky, it stood undamaged, gaudy or gorgeous with its painted frieze, it must have looked entirely different and surely much less to our taste. The nearest we have to an undamaged Hellenic temple must be the Maison Carrée in Nîmes. Granted the pleasing balance of the proportions and the skill involved in the correcting of the proportions; and granted that the Maison Carrée is only a miniature temple, does it not remain true that ancient classical architecture is too massive, too burly for our taste?

But as we have the Parthenon now, a ruin, how beautiful accident has made it, fined down to a few perfectly placed lines.

Our good fortune was to see the Parthenon empty of tourists. We docked at Piraeus at six in the morning; further sleep was impossible because of the noise of cargo being loaded into the holds. As we left the ship the First Officer reminded us that nine o'clock was sailing time and we took a taxi through the wharves and factories of Piraeus, across Athens where already the motor buses were crowded with workers and the road side sellers of bread and rolls were doing a good trade. Up through the Plaka we went and saw housewives cleaning their doorsteps and bundling children out of the house to school.

The Beulé gate was open and a man with a broom waved us in, no bother about money at that hour. We were alone on this great site; we scrambled up the steps, walked through the great temple, feeling the cream coloured stone warm under our hands as the sun rose in the sky. Then down to the Erechtheum all the time talking in hushed voices, for at this time it was truly a holy place.

As we left a minibus drew up and disgorged a dozen or so Americans and Germans with guide book and cine camera at the ready and we realised that we had chosen our time well.

Thackeray to France: February 1849

'It was on the stroke of eleven at night, Sir, on Wednesday the 31st of January, that a traveller might have been perceived plunging rapidly through the shingles of Dover, towards a boat which lay in waiting there, to bear him and other exiles to a steamer which lay in the offing, her slim black hull scarcely visible in the mists of night, through which her lights, of a green and ruby colour, burned brilliantly. The moon was looking out on the fair and tranquil scene, the stars were twinkling in a friendly manner, the ancient cliffs of Albion loomed out of the distant grey. But few lights twinkled in the deserted houses of the terraces along the beach. The bathing machines were gone to roost. There was scarcely a ripple on the sluggish wave as the boat with The Traveller on board went grinding over the shingle, and we pulled to the ship. In fact, the waters of Putney were not more calm than those of the Channel, and the night was as mild as a novel by the last lady of fashion.

'Having paid a shilling for the accommodation of the boat, the traveller stepped on board the deck of the famous steamer *Vivid*, commanded by the intrepid and polite Captain Smithett; and the Mails presently coming off in their boat with the light at its bows, away went the *Vivid* at the rate of seventeen miles an hour, and we were off Calais almost before the second cigar was smoked, or we had had near time enough to think of those beloved beings whom we left behind.

'Sir, there was not enough water in the Calais harbour—so a bawling pilot swore, who came up to us in his lugger; and as she came plunging and bumping against the side of the *Vivid*, Captain Smithett caused the mail-bags first, and afterwards the passengers, to be pitched into her, and we all rolled about amongst the ropes and spars on deck, in the midst of the most infernal bawling and yelling from the crew of Frenchmen, whose howls and contortions, as they got their sail up, and otherwise manoeuvred the vessel, could be equalled by men of no other nation. Some of us were indignant at being called upon to pay three francs for a ride of a mile in this vessel, and declared we would write to the *Times*; but there was One Traveller who had not heard that noise of Frenchmen for four years, and their noise was to his soul as the music of bygone years. That Man, Sir, is perpetually finding something ludicrous in what is melancholy, and when he is most miserable is always most especially jocular.

'Sir, it was the first night of the new Postal arrangement, by which the Mails are made to go from Calais and not from

Boulogne as heretofore. Our goods were whisked through the Custom-House with a rapidity and courtesy highly creditable to Frenchmen, and an enthusiastic omnibus-driver, lashing his horses furiously, and urging them forward with shrieks and howls, brought us to the St. Pierre Station of the railway, where we took our places in the train. 'Twas two in the bleak winter's morn. The engine whistled—the train set forth—we plunged into the country, away, away, away!

'At eleven o'clock, Sir, we dashed into the *enceinte* of the forts that guard the metropolis from foreign invasion, and a few minutes afterwards we were in that dear old Paris that One amongst us had not seen for four years.'

Isambard Kingdom Brunel

Millions of travellers by rail and sea, during the century before the triumph of road over rail and air over sea due to the internal combustion engine, owed the speed and comfort of their going to Isambard Kingdom Brunel, French by birth but English by adoption, more than to any other man in the world. Here, from his *Journal*, is his summing up of the year 1835, when he was twenty-nine:

'The Railway (Great Western) now is in progress. I am their engineer to the finest work in England—a handsome salary— £2000 a year—on excellent terms with my Directors and all going smoothly but what a fight we have had—and how near defeat—and what a ruinous defeat it would have been. It is like looking back upon a fearful pass—but we have succeeded. And it is not this alone but everything I have been engaged in has been successful.

'*Clifton Bridge*—my first child, my darling, is actually going on—recommenced week last Monday—glorious!

'*Sunderland* Docks too going on well—

'*Bristol* Docks. All Bristol is alive and turned bold and speculative with this railway—we are to widen the entrances and Lord knows what.

'*Merthyr and Cardiff* Railway—This too I owe to the G.W.R. I care not, however, about it—

'*Cheltenham Railway*. Of course this I owe to the Great Western —and I may say to myself, Do not feel much interested in this. None of the parties are my friends. I hold it only because they can't do without me—it's an awkward line and the estimate's too low. However, it's all in the way of business and it's a proud thing to monopolise all the West as I do. I must keep it as long as I can but I want *tools*.

'*Bristol and Exeter* Railway—Another too!!

This survey was done in grand style—it's a good line too—and I feel an interest in Bristol to which I owe much—they have stuck well to me. I think we shall carry this Bill—I shall become quite an oracle in Committees of the House . . .

'*Newbury Branch* a little to almost beneath my notice now—it will do as a branch.

'*Suspension Bridge* across the Thames—I have condescended to be engineer to this—but I shant give myself much trouble about it. If done, however, it all adds to my stock of irons.'

There were other Railways in the list. The capital which was to pass through the young man's hands was over five million sterling, worth perhaps fifty millions of our money. No wonder he concluded that entry in his *Journal*, 'I really can hardly believe it when I think of it.'

Brunel was the conceiver and first builder of great trans-Atlantic liners. When he first proposed to build *The Great Western*, he was laughed at. No steamship could possibly carry enough fuel, as well as pay-load, to steam from Europe to America. But Brunel had been doing some arithmetic and had discovered that it was all a matter of daring to build ships big enough. In mathematical terms, he had calculated that whereas the carrying capacity of a hull increased as the cube of its dimensions, the power required to drive it increases only as the square of its dimensions. Of course, there were limiting factors —power of engines as size increased; length of ship and breaking strains etc.; but the point was, the thing was not impossible, it was only a matter of calculating proportions correctly. But only Brunel and a few men who had faith in him realised it. Others, notably that great engineering pundit, Dr. Dionysius Lardner, knew different. The Doctor, addressing the British Association, had his argument pat: 'Take a vessel of 1600 tons provided with 400 horse-power engines. You must take $2\frac{1}{3}$ tons for each horse-power, so the vessel must have 1,348 tons of coal. To that add 400 tons and the vessel must carry a burden of 1,748 tons. I think it would be a waste of time, under all circumstances, to say more to convince you of the inexpediency of attempting a direct voyage to New York . . .' The good doctor had not noticed the difference between a square and a cube.

Brunel's moment of supreme triumph came when *The Great Western*—her main saloon was 75 feet long and 21 feet wide and lavishly furnished with 'ornamental paintings and decorations' steamed into New York 15 days and 5 hours after leaving Bristol, with 200 tons of coal still in her bunkers. James Gordon Bennett recorded this event in what later became *The New York Herald*: 'The approach of the *Great Western* to the harbour, and in front of the Battery, was most magnificent. It was about four o'clock yesterday afternoon. The sky was clear—the crowds immense. The Battery was filled with the human multitude, one half of whom were females, their faces covered with smiles, and their delicate persons with the gayest attire. Below, on the broad blue water, appeared this huge thing of life, with four masts and emitting volumes of smoke. She looked black and black-guard . . . rakish, cool, reckless, fierce and forbidding in sombre colours to an extreme. As she neared the *Sirius*, she slackened her movements, and took a sweep round forming a sort of half circle. At this moment, the whole Battery sent forth a tumultuous shout of delight, at the revelation of her magnificent proportions. After making another turn towards Staten Island, she made another sweep, and shot towards East River with extraordinary speed. The vast multitude rent the air with their shouts again, waving handkerchiefs, hats, hurrahing!'

The Great Western had a displacement of 2,300 tons, was 236 feet long, 35 feet in the beam, had a draft of 16.7 feet. Not much, beside the 85,000 ton monsters of the 'thirties. But for her day, a colossus. Still, Brunel built a bigger ship. He had practically to float a company of his own to undertake it, but *The Great Eastern*, nearly 19,000 tons, 692 feet long, and six times the size of any ship then afloat, was conceived in 1852 and finished in 1857. Brunel had built the great ship in such a way that she had to be launched into the Thames sideways. To add to all the troubles she had given him—a crooked ship-builder John Scott Russell was only one of a hundred—*The Great Eastern* stuck at the first attempt to launch her and as, against his wishes, this had been made a great public occasion, he suffered cruelly at the hands of a hostile press infuriated because, having overdone its praise of the great engineer's boldness and imagination, it had been temporarily cheated of its triumph. A few weeks later, having worked out a method of pushing his great ship into the river by means of hydraulic presses, Brunel launched her in the presence of only his immediate family and his engineers, on the spring tide of Sunday 1 January, 1858. But the physical, mental and moral strain she had cost him was his ruin; neither in pocket nor in health did he ever recover. Sent abroad for his health—he had nephritis and his physician was the Doctor Bright who 'invented' it—he was unable to supervise the completion of his ship and his fellow directors idiotically put themselves into the hands of the scoundrelly Scott Russell again; even after Brunel's death in September 1859, this plausible crook, who looked and talked like an 'eminent Victorian' if ever man did, (whereas Brunel looked like Puck and talked like a genius) tried to claim the credit for Brunel's enormous ship, whereas no man had done more, by scamped work, ignorance and crooked dealing, to hinder her building.

Brunel's service to travelling humanity did not end with the building and launching of this forerunner of the great Cunarders and other 40, 60, 80 thousand ton transatlantic ships. *The Great Eastern*, used as a cable-layer, had a useful life laying cables not only across the Atlantic but all round the world.

Zadar

The first time we saw Zadar was late in the evening when our cargo-passenger ship docked; we dined on board and then went across to the hotel on the sea front for a drink with our friend Mario, one of the *Putnik* chiefs, who was making the trip down the Yugoslav coast. He told us the story of Zadar in the last war, how it was bombed by the allies because the Germans had concentrated their forces there and how when they left they mined part of the town, totally destroying a handsome sea-front boulevard where the rich merchants and ship-owners had lived. We walked around the quiet town and thought it a sad place and steamed out of it at one in the morning.

We liked Yugoslavia and sought a cheap holiday there the next year. We were offered two weeks in Zadar, at the Hotel Borik which was on a peninsula facing the Harbour and the old town. We accepted this suggestion with certain reservations which turned out to be excessive.

Less well known than Dubrovnik or Split, Zadar is one's

ideal of a seaport town. All day the small steamers from up and down the coast and the islands arrive, crowded with passengers, goods and mail. In the early morning the peasants bring their vegetables, goats, handmade baskets, wooden bowls and spoons to the market; later come the business men; on certain days the big excitement is the arrival of the car-ferry from Ancona with its load of Italian, French and English tourists. Later in the day the little steamers take the peasants and business men back to their homes and the town settles into quiet once more.

The great church of St. Donat's stands tall and bare, like a fortress, contrasting oddly with the stark new blocks of flats around it. Built partly on the foundations of a Roman forum it was, when we saw it, surrounded by archaeological excavations. Here and there we saw a fine Roman column or an arch, underfoot a piece of pavement and we hoped that when the site was fully excavated and photographed, the archaeologists would be able to persuade the Government not to build blocks of flats too near to the great church. Yet we realised that Zadar is a working town, a centre for local trade and commerce and they are still making good the war-time devastation to residential property.

Zadar was occupied by the Crusaders in 1203 at the instigation of the Doge of Venice who resented the defeat of his forces in 1180 by the town and its ally, Pisa. Later the Turks tried to take the town and failed. When Napoleon defeated the Venetian Republic the Austrians occupied the whole of Dalmatia and the Istrian peninsula and Zadar remained Austrian until 1918 when the Italians occupied the coast until their defeat in 1943.

Today, old people speak a mixed Italian/Serbo-Croat dialect. Very old waiters in restaurants, which still have the shabby glitter of the Austrian Empire, speak German. Middle-aged people can speak a resentful German imposed upon them in their 1940s youth; school children all want to practise their English: 'Good morning, how are you?' will follow you along the streets when you meet a school 'crocodile'.

Above all, Zadar is a walking town with shady squares and cafés, many churches, some now closed and opened only for tourists if you can find the nun or old lady who has the key. For religion in Yugoslavia is for the old and although there is no overt persecution, if the young wish to make their way in life, they do well to avoid being seen in church. Most important of the churches is the 12th century Romanesque cathedral of Saint Anastasia and here you will be shown around by the *doyenne* of these old ladies who will show you with pride the stone casket in which the remains of Saint Anastasia are buried. You may have difficulty in following her toothless articulation of Italian, spoken at a speed which gains as her enthusiasm increases.

If you are caravanning down the coast and so catering for yourself you will enjoy your visit to the market even more than we did, for the vegetables and meat are of superb quality. We could only buy some small, alpine-type strawberries. These we ate with no ill effects or recourse to medicaments, from the paper bag, and so got the full fragrance which disappears the moment they are washed.

Our hotel, the Borik, was a great find. Set in pinewoods on the edge of the sandy shore of the peninsula, it has a fine bathing beach and, in amongst the trees, a very large auto-camp which we were told is one of the best on the coast for its amenities. Here we found all nationalities, the campers putting up their national flag with as much reverence as the first Moon traveller.

Marianne North

The Marianne North gallery in Kew Gardens contains over eight hundred remarkable paintings of exotic plants and flowers by Marianne North. Miss North, daughter of Frederick North, Liberal M.P. for Hastings, whose friends were people like Sabine, President of the Royal Society from 1861 to 1871; Galton, the scientist; George Bentham, the botanist, and Erskine May, the great constitutional lawyer, was born in 1830 and died in 1890. Twenty of her sixty years were spent in travelling to the most remote and improbable parts of the world to paint flowers, small birds and insects, in a vividly colourful but scientifically accurate style peculiar to her. She was a great success, honoured by the mighty Sir Joseph Hooker of Kew fame, her friendship sought by Charles Darwin.

Her first flower painting journey—in 1871—took her to Canada, the USA, the West Indies, and Brazil. Next, after a season's painting in the Canary Islands, she went by way of California, Japan and Singapore, to Sarawak.

'The Rajah lent me a cook, a soldier, and a boy, gave me a lot of bread, a coopful of chickens, and packed us all into a canoe, in which we pulled through small canals and forest nearly all day; then landed at a village, and walked up 700 feet of beautiful zigzag road, to the clearing in the forest where the farm and chalet were. The view was wonderful from it, with the great swamp stretched out beneath like a ruffled blue sea, the real sea with its islands beyond, and tall giant trees as foreground round the clearing, which was also full of stumps and fallen trees grown over with parasites—the most exquisite velvety and metallic leaves, creeping plants, 'foliage plants', caladiums, alpinias, and the lovely cissu discolor of all manner of colours, creeping over everything . . . Life was very delicious up there. I stayed till I had eaten all the chickens, and the last remains of my bread had turned blue; then . . . I came down, my soldier using his fine long sword to decapitate the leeches which stuck to me by the way.'

From Sarawak she went to Java where she travelled all over the country in carts or on horseback, painting industriously, and from there to Ceylon. After a brief spell in London, she set out again, returning to paint in Ceylon and India, wandering about the Himalayas in a litter carried on the heads of bearers, visiting Rajahs, 'maided' by a gigantic and hideous coolie who used to pick wild flowers for her.

Returning to London to hold the first showing of her pictures, she accepted Charles Darwin's suggestion that she ought to visit Australia, and off she went again, in 1880, staying with Rajah Brooke of Sarawak again, on the way. In carriages and on horseback she covered all Queensland and New South Wales; and Western Australia where the government gave her a police driver, one O'Leary.

'And could get no food, but my Irish police driver boiled his "billy" and made some tea at Black River, where the water was worthy of its name. However, we ate all we had with a better appetite than those who have abundance at home, and divided our few biscuits with Black Johnnie, the policeman's Man Friday, whose Irish was almost as incomprehensible as the language of the natives; but he was very kind to me, and managed to avoid the deep ruts, and to keep the old carriage very cleverly from accidents. It was a kind of "inside car" with two seats sideways—one for myself, one for my portmanteau, and a bit of canvas spread overhead on four poles to keep the sun off. I had a tin biscuit-box half full of damp sand on the floor to put rare flowers in; but the sand soon ceased to be damp, many of the flowers drooped as soon as they were picked, and the whole carriage, as well as the box became full of them. It was impossible not to try to keep the beautiful things for the chance of being able to paint them. At Rogenut I lodged at a police station, and was so surrounded by policemen calling me "your ladyship" that I felt like the Queen of the Cannibal

Islands, and rather a dangerous character. The sundew grew into perfect little trees near there, and we passed a mile of everlasting flowers, one perfect bed of them in the burnt-up grass. Then we came to another marvellous sandy plain, and every kind of small flower—great velvety "kangaroo's feet", with green and yellow linings, exquisite blue or white lobelias, bordering the road like a hedge, and whipping one in the face as the carriage pushed through.'

She visited Tasmania and New Zealand, disliking both places because they were cold, and travelled back to California by way of Honolulu.

Back in London, she built the North Gallery at Kew, to house her paintings, and then, in 1882, set out for Africa in order to complete her collection, travelling up-country by ox-wagon, staying with the famous Bishop Colenso, passing nights in farmhouses, detesting the Boers and contemptuous of the Zulus. From Africa she went to the Seychelles to paint the extraordinary *coco de mer*.

'The stalks forming ornamental points at the corners, and finishing the roof into a curve like the gates of a Japanese temple. There were many of these trees on the island of Curieuse, and a path was cut to one of the biggest, with a pile of boulders behind it, on which I climbed, and perched myself on the top; my friends building up a footstool for me from a lower rock just out of reach. I rested my painting-board on one of the great fan leaves, and drew the whole mass of fruit and buds in perfect security, though the slightest slip or cramp would have put an end both to the sketch and me.'

Her last journey, oppressed by rheumatism and afflicted by head-noises and growing deafness, was to Chile to paint *Araucaria imbricans*, and the great electric blue *Puya*.

Her favourite tree was the gigantic Californian Redwood. She did most of her travelling correctly dressed as a lady and living chiefly on bread and butter; she was kind and good-tempered; she considered the coloured races very inferior to whites and condoned slavery provided it was benevolent. Her life's work, gathered in one place at her Gallery in Kew, should be seen.

Mary Kingsley

Of the women who, in Victorian times, broke all the social shackles which men had bound them with, and overcame such physical difficulties as their very clothes, without yielding an iota of their respectability, in order to travel, Mary Kingsley was the most remarkable. Anthropologist, ethnologist, naturalist and scholar, she was a reformer blessed with a Shavian sense of humour. Born in 1862, during her first thirty years her travelling was restricted to a single journey—to Paris. Even so, she was an eccentric, her circumstances forced her to do the bread-winning by running a magazine.

Her travelling was done between 1893 and 1895 when the European nations were carving up Africa between them. She chose West Africa as her field and went there in a freighter from Liverpool. Here she is in the Mangrove Swamps of the short-lived Oil Rivers Protectorate:
'This is a fascinating pursuit. For people who like that sort of thing it is just the sort of thing they like, as the art critic of a provincial town wisely observed about an impressionist picture recently acquired for the municipal gallery. But it is a pleasure to be indulged in with caution; for one thing you are certain to come across crocodiles ... In addition to this unpleasantness you are liable—until you realize the danger from experience, or have native advice on this point—to get tide-trapped away in the swamps, the water falling round you when you are away in

some deep pool or lagoon and you find you cannot get back to the main river . . . you stop in your lagoon until the tide rises again; most of your attention is directed to dealing with an "at home" to crocodiles and mangrove flies and with the fearful stench of the slime around you. What little time you have over you will employ in wondering why you came to West Africa, and why, after having reached this point of absurdity, you need have gone and painted the lily and adorned the rose, by being such a colossal ass as to come fooling about in mangrove swamps . . . On one occasion a mighty Silurian, as the *Daily Telegraph* would call him, chose to get his front paws over the stern of my canoe and endeavoured to improve our acquaintance. I had to retire to the bows to keep the balance right, and fetch him a clip on the snout with a paddle when he withdrew, and I paddled into the very middle of the lagoon, hoping the water there was too deep for him or any of his friends to repeat the performance.'

Mary Kingsley had a particular taste for the Fan tribe, who were cannibals:

'We each recognized we belonged to that same section of the human race with whom it is better to drink than to fight. We knew we would each have killed the other, if sufficient inducement were offered, and so we took a certain amount of care that the inducement should not arise. Gray Shirt and Pagan also, their trade friends, the Fans treated with an independent sort of courtesy; but Silence, Singlet, the Passenger, and above all Ngouta, they openly did not care a row of pins for, and I have small doubt that had it not been for us other three they would have killed and eaten those amiable gentlemen with as much compunction as an English sportsman would kill as many rabbits. They on their part hated the Fan and never lost an opportunity of telling me "These Fan be bad man too much".'

And here is an account of a meeting between the corseted and bustled traveller and a family of gorillas:

'One old male, one young male, and three females. One of these had clinging to her a young fellow with beautiful wavy black hair with just a kink in it. The big male was crouching on his haunches, with his long arms hanging down on either side, with the backs of his hands on the ground, the palms upwards. The elder lady was tearing to pieces and eating a pine-apple, while the others were at the plantains destroying more than they ate . . . I put out my hand and laid it on Wiki's gun to prevent him from firing, and he, thinking I was going to fire, gripped my wrist. I watched the gorillas with great interest for a few seconds, until I heard Wiki make a peculiar small sound, and looking at him saw his face working in an awful way as he clutched his throat with his hand violently. Heavens! think I, this gentleman's going to have a fit; it's lost we are entirely this time. He rolled his head to and fro, and then buried his face into a heap of dried rubbish at the foot of a plantain stem, clasped his hands over it, and gave an explosive sneeze. The gorillas let go all, raised themselves up for a second, gave a quaint sound between a bark and a howl, and then the ladies and the young gentleman started for home.'

Notes on Travel Drinking

Probably the only place left in the world where drinks are sold at their proper price and untaxed is the Canary Islands. Whisky, 15/- a bottle, gin, 12/-. The native wines are about a shilling a bottle. I have never seen a Canary Islander drunk.

In Brazil Scotch and American whiskies cost about £8 a bottle. At about an eighth of the price, Brazilian whisky is not bad. It never did us any harm. There is a little native wine, made in the relatively cool far south; it would not be bad if better vinified, but as it is it's inclined to be muddy.

Argentine wines from the province of Mendoza are very good, especially some of the reds. But real excellence in wine is attained in Chile whence, if the Chilean *viticulteurs* continue in their present course, I prophesy that great wines will come.

In the United States you can buy Scotch whisky cheaper than in Britain. But liquor laws vary from State to State; in New York, shop around, there is fierce competition between the liquor stores and bargains to be had. In Pennsylvania spirits are sold only from government shops. Virginia prohibits spirits. As for wines, imported European wines are not much dearer than in London. In any case, you can drink native wines. But the only good ones—and those from the Napa Valley are excellent—come from California. For reasons which had to do with the distribution of the aphis *Phylloxera vastatrix* prior to the cultivation of the vine in America, Old World vines could be grown only west of the Rockies. Consequently, east of the Rockies, the vineyards are composed either of native American vines which yield bad wines, or of hybrids whose wine is better but not yet good. We did not begin to find good lists of Californian wines until we got as far west as Missouri; the best lists are in San Francisco.

By our standards all kinds of drink are cheap in Australia. They brew good beer, import and also distil good spirits—Australian brandies are very drinkable—and above all make a great range of good, and a very few excellent wines. Australia could have been a land of great vintages: in 1838 one William Ryne planted a few acres of vines in the Lilydale district, about thirty miles from Melbourne; by 1868, due to the energy and skill of the De Castella brothers, Swiss immigrants, and to a French immigrant, the Baron de Pury, there were 3000 acres. The wines, known as Lilydale Yerings, were, between c. 1890 and 1910, among the world's greatest vintages. Unfortunately the Lilydale region having been made over to dairying and subtopia, these great wines are no more.

Ceylon: drink the best, bottled arak. It is relatively cheap, tastes like *strega* and is perfectly wholesome. European drinks, whether wines or spirits, are very dear and the wines are bad.

Most of India has abandoned prohibition. In Madras you need a liquor permit to buy alcoholic drinks. It is so generous that only an alcoholic could consume his ration. All over India Scotch is exorbitantly dear and so are imported wines where you can get them. Despite warnings, we drank whisky distilled in India. It did us no harm and was palatable.

In the USSR there are no problems for the drinker. Vodka, dear for Soviet citizens, cost two roubles (£1 or $2.40) in the special Berioshka shops where only foreign currency is accepted and where the staff, making deft use of the abacus, are quick at complex currency conversions. Soviet table wines are good and not dear. Ukrainian and Crimean heavy wines are superb and in the Black Sea towns and some Ukrainian towns inland, you can buy a glass of excellent wine—sold by the tumbler—drawn from big barrels on wheels, at street corners. When Soviet citizens celebrate the table is set with wines, beers and small carafes of vodka. To each bumper of wine or beer, they take a chaser, in a minute glass, of vodka: it has a remarkably enlivening effect on their dancing.

In South East Asia you can as a rule and by a careful use of Duty Free shops and the black market in currency, drink whisky, gin or brandy at much less than European prices. Wine is out of the question except for millionaires. In Japan there is *saké*, a kind of rice wine; but it is very insipid.

South Africa is a great wine country and her best wines are excellent, comparable with the Chilean wines. Spirit drinkers are not as harshly treated as in Britain; and wine and food, in this semi-slave economy, are both cheaper than they have any right to be. In East Africa, we drank beer. You can get wines and spirits at the best hotels but only at a high price.

North Africa is too hot in summer to produce really good table wines; it is a mistake to believe that grapes only need lots of sun to produce fine wines; they can have too much. Still, Moroccan and Algerian red wines are drinkable and very cheap.

—And Eating

The despair of our gourmet friends, we may not be the right people to talk about food. At home in England and travelling in Europe we eat small quantities of very concentrated food like meat and fish. We like real bread, green salads and black coffee as strong as only the Italians make it.

Once out of Europe and away from the Channel or Atlantic coast, fish becomes insipid but this is more than compensated for by the excellence of Mediterranean and Adriatic shell fish; oddly enough, we found last year in the south of France that we were eating *Langoustines* brought over from the Dalmatian Coast of Yugoslavia.

In South and Central America the meat is excellent. Juicy fillet steaks; cold roast meat and plenty of salads. In Australia we expected to eat lamb, but found that this is considered a second class food and again, beef is king. They have Pacific prawns and lobsters in abundance. Fish has European names but not the European taste. Our breakfasts were ruined by the coffee; one of the powdered varieties made to the consistency of tea.

In India and Ceylon if you do not like or cannot eat curry, the alternative is the English menu; this consists of the kind of Victorian nursery food that has disappeared from English tables many years ago. Whilst Mary seems to be able to consume hot curries, I found myself doomed to a diet of Brown Windsor Soup, over-cooked mutton or goat with brown gravy or boiled potatoes, followed by Cabinet pudding or a Spotted Dick. Sometimes I would have a small chicken, very tough, but the flavour is excellent. It was about this time that we switched to tea for breakfast, which seemed the sensible thing to do when it is grown on the spot.

In East and South Africa we stayed at such grand hotels that we ate American-type food served in vast quantities, and it was an embarrassment to leave so much on the plate when one knew what the diet of most Africans consists of. But these hotels catered for tourists of all nations; the Germans and Dutch ate every scrap and the Americans are accustomed to only eating a quarter of what they are given. If less had been served complaints would have resulted.

In Russia we expected to eat lots of caviar and found that a small portion in our Moscow hotel cost as much as in England, so we contented ourselves with the menu. We have never eaten so much chicken, nor such strange joints of this bird. It always seemed to us that we got a huge piece, but when you cut into it found that it was the skinny back of the bird and that the breast had gone elsewhere. We had a good Chicken à la Kiev in Kiev; fine, we thought and ordered it in Odessa only to find that it was a sort of rissole cunningly wrapped round a chicken bone. In fact, towards the end of our stay we were on an egg diet and were sometimes very hungry—our own fault, there is plenty of good, heavy, nourishing food to be had, but we lacked the will to eat it.

In North America, of course, there are no problems except again the size of the portions and I refuse to get into arguments about the poor quality of American food. You can always get good salads, bacon and eggs, a steak and fresh fruit, to say nothing of a variety of clams and shell-fish on the Eastern seaboard. And excepting in the poshest places, food is relatively cheap.

One has, of course, to adapt to the local gastronomic customs eating steak accompanied by strong tea in Ireland; cold fried eggs lightly dusted with fluff in Indonesia; getting your meat in shapeless chunks in Brazil; that sort of thing. Our biggest disappointment in the way of food was the insipid taste of tropical fruits: none, with the exception of the pineapple, is as good as the temperate zone fruits.

The traveller who likes Chinese cooking is the happiest. If there is anywhere in the world where you cannot get it, I don't know where it can be.

I enjoy Baedekers, Guides Michelin, Guides Bleus and the rest. I especially enjoy the more recondite items of information one occasionally finds in them. Here, for instance, from the *1969 Fodor Guide to Greece*, is a case in point; on the subject of Corfu:

'A Russian general was the first to rediscover the serenity of the wooded promontory, and instead of a gun emplacement he built himself a pavilion. It would be going too far to say that this aesthetic indulgence led to the loss of the island, but soon afterwards the second Lord High Commissioner outshone his Russian predecessor by presenting the villa of Mon Repos, surrounded by a beautiful park, to his bearded spouse. "Sir Frederick's Folly" passed later into the possession of the Greek royal family.'

Who, I wonder, can this unusual lady have been.

NOTE: The Puzzle for Sailors is from Swift's A voyage to Brobdingnag. It is complete nonsense.

Index

Index

of, growing around Greek temples, 18; wines, 244–5; young cricketers, 42–3
Austria, traffic noise in, 40
'Automan' described, 23–6
Avanti, ancient holy city of India, 91
Ayodya, ancient holy city of India, 91
Aztec city building, 160

Bachmann-Naegli, Mrs., 58–9
Badogra military airport, north of Calcutta, 73
Balsa rafts, 108, 109
Bani Kaab tribe, Oman, 152
Bar customs, 217–19
Barbarossa, the Emperor, 176
Barberries growing wild, 112
Bargaining, in Italian street markets, 163
Barrancos of Canaries, 208
Barsac country, 146
Baseball, 43–4
Basques, 199
Batavia, 123
Beggars, 221–3
Belgium, traffic noise and careless driving in, 40
Bengal, *see* Tibetan refugees
Bennett, James Gordon, on arrival of *Great Western* in New York, 233
Bentham, George, 238
Berberis darwinii, 96
Bergerac, 147
Berlin and Munich, road manners in, 40
Betel chewing, 32
de Bethencourt, Jean, first conqueror of the Canaries, 98, 99, 187–9

Bissardon and Bony, tapestry by, 58
Blue (also Green, Red) champagne circuits, 145
Blue Mountains, Virginia, 216
de Bobadilla, Beatriz, and Ferdinand of Aragon, 207
Boccaccio, description of Fortunate Islands by, 1341, 98–9
Body-line bowling, 42
Boeklin, Arnold (*Toteninsel*), 165
Bogor, Java, 78–9; the *Hortus Bogoriensis*, 80
Bolsena, a miracle at, 175
Bombay, 135
Bonnano, architect of Leaning Tower of Pisa, 227
Bontier, Pierre, and Le Verrier, Jean, on J. de Bethencourt, 188–9
Books: Argentine, 50; Australian Customs and, 85; France, 50–2
Bordeaux, 146, 147
Boston, Mass.: Customs, 22–3
Botanising on horseback, 216
Bourgueil wine country, 148
Brazil (*see also* Rio de Janeiro); Customs, 86; drink prices, 243–4; some butterflies of, 169
Brick earths, connection with good fruit, 89
Bright, Dr., and Bright's disease, 234
Bristol Docks, Bristol and Exeter Railway, Bristol Suspension Bridge, works of Brunel, 232
British Isles, discovery of, 226–7
Brooke, Rajah, of Sarawak, Marianne North stays with, 239
Brown, 'Capability', 61–2
Brunel, Isambard K., 231–5

Index

Index

Index

257

Index

Index

Index

Index

Urban IV, Pope, and Orvieto cathedral, 175

U.S.A. (*see also* named cities): 'automan', 23–6; 'Customs', 87; drink prices, liquor laws, 244; motels, 216–17; night-walking, 220–1; pre-1920 book piracy, 215

U.S.S.R. (*see also* named cities), 15–20, 122–3, 219; art, 19, 72; beach life, 69; bourgeois nature of society, 142–3; 'Customs', 86; children's summer holidays, 67–8; cigarettes, 71; cost of caviar, 71; dancing, 71–2; and deaths of foreign public figures, 202–3; flying (internal), 66, 206; food, 71, 247, 248; gypsies, 33–4; health service, 117–18; holiday areas, 65–73; holidays, five types of 66–7; hotels, 34–5; ice cream, 73; latitudes affecting manners, 119; legacies, 142–4; monuments, 19–20; music, 72; public transport, 205–6; urban scene, 14–15; wines, 70, 71, 245

Uzbekistan, 1963 earthquake in, 189–90

Vann-Bree, portrait of Napoleon by, 58

Venice and Leiden, canals of, compared, 40

Vernet, Horace, portrait of Napoleon by, 59

Verona, fruit-growing areas of, 89

Vienna, traffic noise of, 40

Vigneron, P. R., portrait of Napoleon by, 58

Vignola, architect to Cardinal Gambara, 182

Villa Lante, near Viterbo, 182–3

Villarca (peak of Andes), 100

Vine brought to Mexico, 103

Vishnu, worship of, 38, 39, 92

Vodka, 245

Volterra, 173; Etruscan Museum in, 174

'Vopos', East Germany, 136–8

Vouvray wine country, 148, 149

Waitangi, Treaty of, 124

Water, cities built in, 159–61

Westphalia, Humphry Repton in, 186–7

Williams, Mrs. Victoria, of Himalaya Hotel, 77

Wines: for travellers, 104–5; of Argentine, 244; of Australia, 244–5; of Canaries, 243; of Chile, 244; France's wine rivers, 145–7; in India, 245; in Mexico, 102–3; of Russia, 70–1, 245; of S. Africa and N. Africa, 246; of S.E. Asia, 245; of U.S.A., 244. *See also* Burgundy

Xavier, St. Francis, 220, 221

Xochimilcho, Lake, 160

Yalta, 210; Chekov Theatre in, 72; Nikitsy Sad (botanic garden), 203; Yalta to Livadia coast, 65–73, 117–18

Yemen, medicine in the, 150–1

Yugoslavia, 192–4; gypsies of, 33–4; *langoustines of*, 246; *see* Zadar

Yupanqui, Topa Inca, 108–9

Zadar, Yugoslavia, 235–7

Zen Buddhist gardens, 224–5

Zopilote (Mexican birds), 168–9